W9-AUI-683

OPPOSING
VIEWPOINTS®
SERIES

Cloning

Other Books of Related Interest:

Opposing Viewpoints Series

Alternative Medicine

Population

Stem Cells

At Issue Series

Are Mass Extinctions Inevitable?

DNA Databases

The Ethics of Medical Testing

Current Controversies Series

Human Genetics

Medical Ethics

"Congress shall make
no law ... abridging
the freedom of speech,
or of the press."

First Amendment to the US Constitution

The basic foundation of our democracy is the First Amendment guarantee of freedom of expression. The Opposing Viewpoints series is dedicated to the concept of this basic freedom and the idea that it is more important to practice it than to enshrine it.

Cloning

Jacqueline Langwith, Book Editor

GREENHAVEN PRESS
A part of Gale, Cengage Learning

Detroit • New York • San Francisco • New Haven, Conn • Waterville, Maine • London

GALE
CENGAGE Learning

Elizabeth Des Chenes, *Managing Editor*

For more information, contact:
Greenhaven Press
27500 Drake Rd.
Farmington Hills, MI 48331-3535
Or you can visit our Internet site at gale.cengage.com

For product information and technology assistance, contact us at

Gale Customer Support, 1-800-877-4253
For permission to use material from this text or product, submit all requests online at www.cengage.com/permissions

Further permissions questions can be emailed to permissionrequest@cengage.com

Articles in Greenhaven Press anthologies are often edited for length to meet page requirements. In addition, original titles of these works are changed to clearly present the main thesis and to explicitly indicate the author's opinion. Every effort is made to ensure that Greenhaven Press accurately reflects the original intent of the authors. Every effort has been made to trace the owners of copyrighted material.

Cover Image © Pictor International/ImageState/Alamy.

LIBRARY OF CONGRESS CATALOGING-IN-PUBLICATION DATA

Cloning / Jacqueline Langwith, book editor.
    p. cm. -- (Opposing viewpoints)
    Includes bibliographical references and index.
    ISBN 978-0-7377-5713-2 (hbk.) -- ISBN 978-0-7377-5714-9 (pbk.)
    1. Cloning--Juvenile literature. 2. Cloning--Moral and ethical aspects--Juvenile literature. I. Langwith, Jacqueline.
    QH442.2.C56475 2012
    176'.22--dc23

           2011051020

Printed in the United States of America
1 2 3 4 5 6 7 16 15 14 13 12

Contents

Why Consider Opposing Viewpoints?

"The only way in which a human being can make some approach to knowing the whole of a subject is by hearing what can be said about it by persons of every variety of opinion and studying all modes in which it can be looked at by every character of mind. No wise man ever acquired his wisdom in any mode but this."

John Stuart Mill

In our media-intensive culture it is not difficult to find differing opinions. Thousands of newspapers and magazines and dozens of radio and television talk shows resound with differing points of view. The difficulty lies in deciding which opinion to agree with and which "experts" seem the most credible. The more inundated we become with differing opinions and claims, the more essential it is to hone critical reading and thinking skills to evaluate these ideas. Opposing Viewpoints books address this problem directly by presenting stimulating debates that can be used to enhance and teach these skills. The varied opinions contained in each book examine many different aspects of a single issue. While examining these conveniently edited opposing views, readers can develop critical thinking skills such as the ability to compare and contrast authors' credibility, facts, argumentation styles, use of persuasive techniques, and other stylistic tools. In short, the Opposing Viewpoints Series is an ideal way to attain the higher-level thinking and reading skills so essential in a culture of diverse and contradictory opinions.

In addition to providing a tool for critical thinking, Opposing Viewpoints books challenge readers to question their own strongly held opinions and assumptions. Most people form their opinions on the basis of upbringing, peer pressure, and personal, cultural, or professional bias. By reading carefully balanced opposing views, readers must directly confront new ideas as well as the opinions of those with whom they disagree. This is not to argue simplistically that everyone who reads opposing views will—or should—change his or her opinion. Instead, the series enhances readers' understanding of their own views by encouraging confrontation with opposing ideas. Careful examination of others' views can lead to the readers' understanding of the logical inconsistencies in their own opinions, perspective on why they hold an opinion, and the consideration of the possibility that their opinion requires further evaluation.

Evaluating Other Opinions

To ensure that this type of examination occurs, Opposing Viewpoints books present all types of opinions. Prominent spokespeople on different sides of each issue as well as well-known professionals from many disciplines challenge the reader. An additional goal of the series is to provide a forum for other, less known, or even unpopular viewpoints. The opinion of an ordinary person who has had to make the decision to cut off life support from a terminally ill relative, for example, may be just as valuable and provide just as much insight as a medical ethicist's professional opinion. The editors have two additional purposes in including these less known views. One, the editors encourage readers to respect others' opinions—even when not enhanced by professional credibility. It is only by reading or listening to and objectively evaluating others' ideas that one can determine whether they are worthy of consideration. Two, the inclusion of such viewpoints encourages the important critical thinking skill of objectively evaluating an author's credentials and bias. This evaluation will illuminate an author's reasons for taking a particular stance on an issue and will aid in readers' evaluation of the author's ideas.

It is our hope that these books will give readers a deeper understanding of the issues debated and an appreciation of the complexity of even seemingly simple issues when good and honest people disagree. This awareness is particularly important in a democratic society such as ours in which people enter into public debate to determine the common good. Those with whom one disagrees should not be regarded as enemies but rather as people whose views deserve careful examination and may shed light on one's own.

Thomas Jefferson once said that "difference of opinion leads to inquiry, and inquiry to truth." Jefferson, a broadly educated man, argued that "if a nation expects to be ignorant and free . . . it expects what never was and never will be." As individuals and as a nation, it is imperative that we consider the opinions of others and examine them with skill and discernment. The Opposing Viewpoints series is intended to help readers achieve this goal.

David L. Bender and Bruno Leone,
Founders

Introduction

"The ability to routinely write the 'software of life' will usher in a new era in science, and with it, new products and applications such as advanced biofuels, clean water technology, food products, and new vaccines and medicines."

—J. Craig Venter,
American pioneer in genomic research

On May 20, 2010, an article appeared in the online version of the prestigious *Science* magazine announcing the creation of man-made life. Led by J. Craig Venter, a team of researchers reported "the design, synthesis, and assembly" of a modified version of a bacteria that typically lives in the lungs of cattle and goats. On the same day that Venter's article was published, President Barack Obama requested that the newly formed Presidential Commission for the Study of Bioethical Issues (PCSBI) look at the ethical implications of "synthetic biology," the field of science encompassing Venter's bacterial creation. A week later, a US congressional committee held a hearing on the same topic. The significant interest in synthetic biology lies in its extraordinary potential to benefit mankind. However, like cloning, synthetic biology has many ethical concerns. What is synthetic biology? The website SyntheticBiology .org, created by students and faculty members at Harvard University and the Massachusetts Institute of Technology, asserts that synthetic biology refers to both:

- the design and fabrication of biological components and systems that do not already exist in the natural world, and

- the redesign and fabrication of existing biological systems.

English scientists Andrew Balmer and Paul Martin offer a simpler explanation for synthetic biology. According to the scientists, synthetic biology is "the deliberate design of biological systems and living organisms using engineering principles."[1] Still, another explanation of synthetic biology, provided by the PCSBI, contrasts synthetic biology with standard biology. According to the PCSBI, "whereas standard biology treats the structure and chemistry of living things as natural phenomena to be understood and explained, synthetic biology treats biochemical processes, molecules, and structures as raw materials and tools to be used in novel and potentially useful ways, often quite independent of their natural roles."[2]

Synthetic biology has been made possible through advances in scientists' knowledge about genes and by the availability of advanced technologies that allow scientists to manipulate genes in the laboratory. Each year since James Watson and Francis Crick described the structure of DNA in 1953, scientists' knowledge of genes has steadily risen. From the early knowledge that genes are composed of varying sequences of four different molecules of DNA—adenosine (A), thymine (T), cytosine (C), and guanine (G)—scientists have been able to elucidate the entire genetic sequence of several living organisms, including humans. Today, scientists use gene synthesizers to either replicate gene sequences found in nature or to create novel genes by stitching As, Ts, Cs, and Gs together in ways not found in nature.

To make their synthetic bacteria, Venter and his team replicated genes from a bacterium called *Mycoplasma mycoides*, which causes lung infections in cattle and goats. After tweaking some of the genes to create new sequences, they then transplanted them into an enucleated cell (a cell with its nucleus removed) of a closely related bacterium. An article in the *Economist* highlighting the importance of this achievement said that Venter had "created a living creature with no ancestor" and a "Rubicon had been crossed." According to the

Economist, "synthetic biology makes it possible to conceive of a world in which new bacteria (and eventually, new animals and plants) are designed on a computer and then grown to order." This ability says the *Economist*, "would prove mankind's mastery over nature in a way more profound than even the detonation of the first atomic bomb."[3]

Venter's work and other applications of synthetic biology so far have involved the creation of novel microorganisms, particularly medicine-producing and fuel-producing microbes. For instance, synthetic biology is being used to produce the antimalarial drug artemisinin. According to the World Health Organization (WHO), artemisinin-based combination therapy is the best treatment available for malaria, a disease that kills millions of people in the developing world every year. Artemisinin is produced naturally by the plant *Artemisia annua*. However, the plant is hard to grow and artemisinin yields are low. These factors led synthetic biologist Jay Keasling from the University of California, Berkeley, to focus his research on the creation of microbes that can quickly and inexpensively produce bulk quantities of artemisinin. In a 2009 article about Keasling's artemisinin project in the *New Yorker* magazine, Michael Specter noted that "Keasling realized that the tools of synthetic biology, if properly deployed, could dispense with nature entirely, providing an abundant new source of artemisinin." Keasling also told Specter that artemisinin shouldn't be the end of the story, "we ought to be able to make any compound produced by a plant inside a microbe . . . you need this drug: O.K., we pull this piece, this part, and this one off the shelf. You put them into a microbe, and two weeks later out comes your product."[4]

At the congressional hearings on synthetic biology, Keasling also described another important application of synthetic biology with which he is involved. Keasling is the chief executive officer and vice president of the Fuels Synthesis Division at the Joint BioEnergy Institute (JBEI) in Emeryville, California. Researchers at the JBEI are exploring the potential of synthetic biology to produce plant-based fuels, i.e., biofuels, which can replace gasoline and other transportation fuels. The JBEI researchers have been developing procedures to produce these biofuels from Keasling's novel artemisinin-producing microbe. Keasling and his team at the JBEI hope to produce enough biofuels to make a significant dent in the United States' reliance on foreign sources of oil.

The production of medicines and biofuels using engineered microorganisms may not seem frightening. However, many people looking beyond these initial applications see synthetic biology as deeply troubling research. In its report, the PCSBI noted that synthetic biology's critics "express concerns about 'playing God,' threatening biodiversity and the organization and natural history of species, demeaning and disrespecting the meaning of life, and threatening long-standing concepts of nature."[5]

In 2008 the Hastings Center, a nonpartisan, nonprofit bioethics research institute, began a project to examine the ethical concerns about synthetic biology. Gregory E. Kaebnick, a research scholar at the center and one of the lead researchers on the project, testified at the US congressional hearings on synthetic biology. According to Kaebnick, synthetic biology raises two different types of concerns. First, it raises concerns about potential risks and consequences to the natural world of creating new life-forms. Second, it raises intrinsic concerns dealing with whether or not the creation of synthetic organisms is a good or a bad thing in and of itself, aside from the consequences. These intrinsic concerns, according to Kaebnick, are the same concerns many people have about reproductive cloning. They feel it is wrong, regardless of the benefits.

Many of the ethical concerns about synthetic biology were expressed in the days after Venter's May 20, 2010, *Science* article was published. Several media reports from the United

States and England contained quotes from ethics professor Julian Savulescu, from the University of Oxford, and David King, director of the organization Human Genetics Alert. Savulescu said, "Venter is creaking open the most profound door in humanity's history, potentially peeking into its destiny. He is not merely copying life artificially or modifying it by genetic engineering. He is going towards the role of God. Creating artificial life that could never have existed." David King said, "What is really dangerous is these scientists' ambitions for total and unrestrained control over nature, which many people describe as 'playing God.'"[6] Christian commentator Chuck Colson elaborated on King's thoughts by adding, "even if our intentions are pure and our standards are rigorous, we humans are neither as smart nor as competent as our God-like pretensions make us feel. Fallen, finite man often finds ways to turn yesterday's nightmare scenario into tomorrow's headline. In a world where bridges collapse, oil rigs blow up, and cars suddenly accelerate, God-like control isn't only hubris, it's pure fantasy. The only real way to avoid the unthinkable is not to try and play God in the first place. But that would require the kind of humility that Venter and company reject out-of-hand."[7]

In an interview with the BBC on the day his article was published, Venter responded to critics' claims that he was playing God. According to Venter, the term "playing God" comes up every time there is a new medical or scientific breakthrough associated with biology. But says Venter, "'playing God' has been a goal of humanity from the earlier stages to try to control nature—that's how we got domesticated animals. This is the next stage in our understanding. It is a baby step in our understanding of how life fundamentally works and maybe how we can get some new handles on trying to control these microbial systems to benefit humanity."[8]

A year later, Venter was still getting asked whether he was "playing God." In a story for *60 Minutes* in June 2011, Steve

Kroft asked Venter whether he was acting with hubris and was irresponsible as some had charged. Venter responded, "I can tell you what we're doing is safe. There's no way that I can guarantee that other people that use these tools will do intelligent, safe experiments with it. But I think the chance of evil happening with this and somebody even trying to do deliberate evil would be pretty hard." Kroft then asked Venter if he was "playing God," and Venter responded, "We're not playing anything. We're understanding the rules of life."[9]

Synthetic biology has not elicited the same kind of response that cloning has from the religious community. Unlike cloning, to which the religious community is generally vehemently opposed, synthetic biology has some support. For instance, theologian Nancey Murphy from the Fuller Theological Seminary in Pasadena, California, was quoted in the *Wall Street Journal* as saying that synthetic biology "is very much within divine mandate."[10] Furthermore, an article in the national Catholic weekly magazine *America* attributed the Vatican newspaper *L'Osservatore Romano* as saying, "Venter's creation has produced 'an interesting result,' which could have many applications, but the new technology 'must have rules just like everything that lies at the heart of life.'" The *America* article also quoted Cardinal Angelo Bagnasco, president of the Italian bishops' conference, as saying that the development of the first synthetic cell was a "further sign of human intelligence, which is a great gift of God." However, with intelligence comes responsibility, he said. Therefore, any intellectual or scientific advancement "must always measure up to an ethical standard."[11]

As synthetic biology expands and scientists' achievements are registered, the ethical concerns surrounding this field will likely increase as well. However, it is questionable whether ethical concerns of synthetic biology will achieve the same level that cloning has, unless scientists try to recreate human life. Biotechnological advances that can be seen as meddling in the creation of human life generally elicit the most passionate debates. In *Opposing Viewpoints: Cloning*, scientists, theologians, ethicists, legal scholars, and many others contribute their thoughts on the controversial issue of cloning.

Notes

1. Andrew Balmer and Paul Martin, "Synthetic Biology Social and Ethical Challenges," Biotechnology and Biological Sciences Research Council, May 2008.
2. Presidential Commission for the Study of Bioethical Issues, *New Directions: The Ethics of Synthetic Biology and Emerging Technologies*, Washington, DC, December 2010.
3. *Economist*, "Synthetic Biology: And Man Made Life," May 20, 2010.
4. Michael Specter, "A Life of Its Own," *New Yorker*, September 28, 2009.
5. Presidential Commission for the Study of Bioethical Issues, December 2010.
6. Richard Alleyne, "Scientist Craig Venter Creates Life for First Time in Laboratory Sparking Debate About 'Playing God,'" *Telegraph*, May 20, 2010.
7. Chuck Colson, "Synthetic Life: The Danger of God-Like Pretensions," Breakpoint.org, June 14, 2010. www.break point.org.
8. Victoria Gill, "'Artificial Life' Breakthrough Announced by Scientists," BBC News, May 21, 2010.
9. *60 Minutes*, "Designing Life: What's Next for J. Craig Venter?," June 12, 2011.
10. Robert Lee Hotz, "Scientists Create Synthetic Organism," *Wall Street Journal*, May 21, 2010.
11. *America*, "Vatican Greets First Synthetic Cell with Caution," June 7, 2010.

CHAPTER 1

What Ethical and Moral Issues Surround Research Cloning?

Chapter Preface

Support groups generally abound for those who suffer from cancer, multiple sclerosis, cerebral palsy, and other common diseases and disorders. However, when individuals or those they love are diagnosed with an obscure disease, support groups are more difficult to find. Such is typically the case when a mitochondrial disease is diagnosed, such as Alpers' disease or MELAS (mitochondrial myopathy, encephalopathy, lactic acidosis, and stroke) syndrome. Mitochondrial diseases often strike children and young adults and can cause a range of debilitating conditions, such as muscle weakness, blindness, brain disorders, liver failure, heart problems, and even death. As the name implies, these diseases are caused by defects to a person's mitochondria, generally brought about by damaged DNA either within the mitochondria itself or within nuclear genes that facilitate proper mitochondrial function. In April 2010, American researchers successfully carried out a procedure that might someday be used to eradicate those diseases that are caused by defective DNA within the mitochondria itself. The procedure, called mitochondrial swapping, appears promising. However, like cloning and other advanced biotechnologies, it is fraught with ethical concerns.

Mitochondria are organelles in animal cells that function like tiny power plants. In most middle and high school biology courses, students learn that one of the important differences between animal cells and bacterial cells is that animal cells contain organelles, while bacterial cells do not. Organelles carry out very specific functions within a cell. For instance, the nucleus is an organelle that houses most of the cell's DNA and directs all the functions of the cell. The ribosome is an organelle that manufactures the proteins the cell needs to function. Mitochondria are organelles that produce energy—in the form of the chemical adenosine triphosphate, or ATP—

that the cell needs to function. These "cellular batteries," as they are often called, contain their own small piece of DNA, separate from the DNA that is found in the nucleus.

Scientists didn't know that mitochondria contained DNA until 1963. That was when husband and wife researchers in Sweden first visualized mitochondrial DNA while examining the mitochondria of chick embryos under an electron microscope. Since then, scientists have learned that each mitochondrion in a human cell contains thirty-seven genes, all of which are inherited solely from the mother.

Some twenty-five years after scientists learned about mitochondrial DNA, they realized the important role it can play in causing human disease. In 1988 mitochondrial geneticist Douglas Wallace discovered that a single mutation in mitochondrial DNA caused Leber hereditary optic neuropathy (LHON), a disease causing blindness in young men. Also that year, other diseases were linked to defective mitochondrial DNA. Since then, scientists have discovered that many diseases are caused by defects in mitochondrial DNA.

Professor Doug Turnbull, from Newcastle University in the United Kingdom, has been studying mitochondrial diseases for many years. One aspect of Turnball's research is focused on trying to prevent the transmission of these diseases from mother to child.

In April 2010, Turnball and his associates published a paper in the journal *Nature* that demonstrated that mitochondrial disease can in fact be prevented using a technique dubbed mitochondrial swapping. In the technique—which is similar to cloning, or somatic cell nuclear transfer—the nucleus of a fertilized human egg cell that has not yet begun to divide and develop is extracted and transferred to an enucleated egg cell, i.e., an egg cell with its nucleus removed. The resulting human embryo will carry the DNA of three people—the mother and father who created the fertilized egg cell and the woman who donated the enucleated egg cell.

In a story about Turnball's research published by Reuters on April 14, 2010, Turnbull said that he hoped the first babies free from mitochondrial diseases would be born within three years. Turnbull told Reuters' Ben Hirschler that "a child born using this method would have correctly functioning mitochondria, but in every other respect would get all their genetic information from their father and mother."[1]

Not everyone is happy with Turnbull's research, however. Some people say the technique is a form of human genetic engineering that crosses an ethical line. Father Tadeusz Pacholczyk from the Catholic Education Resource Center is one who believes mitochondrial DNA swapping should not be done. He believes there are at least two ethical concerns associated with the procedure. First, he believes that it will encourage the use of artificial reproductive methods, like *in-vitro* fertilization, which he believes is an inherently unethical approach to human reproduction. Second, he believes mitochondrial swapping would "introduce a rupture into parenthood, by creating children who inherit genetic material from three parents." According to Father Pacholczyk, "we are not actually 'repairing' a defective egg, but constructing a new, alternative, and clearly different egg out of the contributions from two separate women. The final egg produced really belongs to neither woman, so that the technological manipulations introduce a fissure between any child conceived from the engineered egg and both 'mothers.'"[2] Douglas Wallace, the mitochondrial geneticist who linked defective mitochondrial DNA to LHON in 1988, disagrees with Father Pacholczyk. In an article by Brandon Keim published by *Wired*, Wallace asked rhetorically, "is it fair for society to make it impossible for a woman who has a high percentage of mutant mitochondrial issues to have a healthy baby? That's what I'm confronted with in my clinic," he said. "There's an ethic of what's best for the patient."[3]

As Wallace suggests, looking for cures and trying to help patients is a driving force behind the development of advanced biotechnological procedures such as mitochondrial swapping. Cloning for research purposes was also developed with the goal of trying to cure devastating diseases. Many scientists are hopeful that research cloning can help cure diseases like diabetes and can help people with spinal cord injuries walk again. However, like mitochondrial swapping, research cloning is fraught with many ethical and moral concerns. These concerns are debated and discussed by the contributors in the following chapter of *Opposing Viewpoints: Cloning.*

Notes

1. Ben Hirschler, "DNA Egg Swap Prevents Rare Diseases in Babies," Reuters, April 14, 2010.
2. Tadeusz Pacholczyk, "The Ethics of 'Correcting' Mitochondrial Disease," National Catholic Bioethics Center, September 2009.
3. Brandon Keim, "3-Parent Embryos Could Prevent Disease, but Raise Ethical Issues," *Wired*, April 14, 2010.

> *"If it is permissible to use embryos in research in the course of which it is known that they will be destroyed, why should it not be permissible as well to create them for that purpose by means that are not intrinsically immoral."*

Research Cloning Is Ethical

Dan W. Brock

In the following viewpoint, medical ethicist Dan W. Brock argues that there are no morally compelling reasons against using cloning to create human embryos solely for utilization in stem cell research. Brock says that human embryos are not full moral persons, and therefore, their use and destruction in important stem cell research is ethical. He also contends that creating embryos using in vitro fertilization (IVF) for research purposes is ethical; it is equivalent to using IVF to help couples have children. Brock asserts that if embryonic stem cell research and IVF are moral, then using cloning to create embryos for stem cell research is also moral. Brock is a professor of medical ethics at Harvard Medical School and the director of the Harvard University Program in Ethics and Health.

Dan W. Brock, "Creating Embryos for Use in Stem Cell Research," *Journal of Law, Medicine and Ethics*, vol. 38, no. 2, Summer 2010, pp. 229–237. Copyright © 2010 by Wiley-Blackwell. All rights reserved. Reproduced by permission.

As you read, consider the following questions:

1. According to Brock, there are at least two different versions of opposition to the use of human embryos in stem cell research. What does he call the view that holds that a human embryo may not be a full human person, but it still has moral status?

2. Which version of the "nothing is lost" principle does Brock say applies to surplus embryos from IVF? Does Brock think this version is defensible?

3. According to Brock, what is a human embryo, if one assumes that it "is not a person with full moral status, or a being with intermediate moral status incompatible with its destruction"?

The intense and extensive debate over human embryonic stem cell (hESC) research has focused primarily on the moral status of the human embryo. Some commentators assign full moral status of normal adult human beings to the embryo from the moment of its conception. At the other extreme are those who believe that a human embryo has no significant moral status at the time it is used and destroyed in stem cell research. And in between are many intermediate positions that assign an embryo some degree of moral status between none and full. This controversy and the respective positions, like the abortion controversy, are by now well understood, despite the lack of progress in resolving it. I have argued briefly elsewhere that early embryos do not have significant moral status, but I do not want to reenter that debate here. Instead, I want to focus on an issue that has had relatively little explicit and separate attention, but is likely to loom larger in light of the [Barack] Obama administration's partial lifting of the [George W.] Bush administration's restriction on the embryos that can be used in stem cell research that receives federal funding.

The rationale offered for the Bush policy had been that if only research using stem cell lines that already existed at the time the policy was announced could receive federal funding, there would be no incentive for any further destruction of embryos. The life and death decision had already been made for any embryos used to create already existing stem cell lines. The new [March 9, 2009] Obama administration policy apparently allows funding for stem cells created by the use of surplus embryos left over from in vitro fertilisation (IVF) undertaken for reproductive purposes, but retains the restriction against federal funding of hESC research using embryos created specifically for use in research. These embryos might be created by IVF in the absence of any reproductive intent, or by somatic cell nuclear transfer (SCNT) if and when that becomes possible. (Laws in some states, such as Massachusetts, also explicitly prohibit the use of embryos created for research, but other states permit it and these policies and laws are always subject to change.) This new policy is likely to focus attention on the putative moral difference between these so-called surplus embryos from IVF and embryos created explicitly for use in research. In this [viewpoint] I will address whether this restriction on the creation of human embryos solely for the purpose of research in which they will be used and destroyed in the creation of human stem cell lines is ethically justified. . . .

Destruction of Embryos Solely for the Purpose of Research

Some people, of course, oppose the creation and destruction of human embryos for research because they oppose any deliberate destruction of human embryos, however and for whatever purpose those embryos were created or used. There are at least two different versions of this view. On the first version, as noted above, human embryos are held to be full human persons with all the moral protections against being deliberately harmed or destroyed that all other persons possess. If an entity is a full human person, its moral status does not depend on how or for what purpose it was created. An infant, child, or adult created by IVF, for example, is no less a full human person than one created by ordinary sexual intercourse. In this version of the opposition to destroying human embryos, the issue is whether a human embryo is a full human person. As stated above, I shall not pursue this issue here. For the purposes of this [viewpoint], I shall assume that human embryos are not full human persons with the moral status that would entail in order to focus on the issue of creating embryos specifically and only for use in stem cell research in which they will be destroyed.

In the second version of this opposition to the use of human embryos in hESC research, the human embryo is not held to be a full human person, but neither is it mere human tissue with no moral status. Instead, in this view a human embryo has what I have elsewhere called "intermediate moral status." It is neither a full human person, nor like mere human tissue with no moral status. In this view, usually because of its membership in the human species or its potential to develop into a person, the embryo is morally owed a certain respect, even if not all the moral protections of a full human person. Of course, the idea of intermediate moral status is vague with regard to the degree of moral status, and the specific moral protections and respect that status requires. Some hold, indeed think it obvious, that deliberately killing or destroying a living being is clearly incompatible with showing it this moral respect. In particular, it is incompatible with respecting the human embryo to destroy it in the service of the development of stem cell lines. In stating the case against cloning for stem cell research, the President's Council on Bioethics stated "that it is incoherent and self-contradictory ... to claim that embryos deserve 'special respect' and to endorse nonetheless research that requires the creation, use, and destruction of these organisms." Now for the moment, ignore the "creation" in this quote and focus only on the use or destruction. It is correct that it is certainly not the typical way that we show respect for either a thing, such as a statute, or an organism, such as an animal or a human person, to deliberately destroy it.

Nevertheless, I believe and have argued elsewhere that it is a mistake to think that intermediate moral status requiring special respect is incompatible with the use and deliberate destruction of embryos in research. Consider another type of entity to which many persons assign intermediate moral status—animals such as monkeys or dogs. These animals are not mere things to be used for human purposes in any way we wish; their capacity to suffer, at a minimum, undergirds their intermediate moral status. Yet these animals are used and sometimes killed or destroyed in the course of biomedical research aimed at understanding and treating serious human disease. Many people accept that practice as morally permissible and compatible with the animals' significant, but intermediate, moral status. Yet many of those same people typically oppose the use and destruction of such animals for cosmetics research. What is the difference? It is clearly and only the seriousness or importance of the purposes of the two activities. It is incompatible with these animals' intermediate moral status and the special respect they are owed to use and destroy them for a relatively trivial human purpose such as developing cosmetics. Limiting their use and destruction only to research aimed at understanding and treating or preventing serious human disease and suffering is a way of showing them special respect and recognizing that their intermediate moral status implies that they are not mere things and so cannot be used for just any human purpose, or in any way that would serve some human purpose.

Likewise, human embryos could be shown the special respect that intermediate moral status requires by limiting their use to comparably important human purposes. That special respect would justify guidelines limiting embryos' use and destruction to research with reasonable promise of alleviating serious human disease and suffering, together with procedures to ensure that those guidelines were followed. There is little controversy that hESC research has that promise, despite uncertainty about how likely or quickly that promise may be realized. Currently, IRB [institutional review board, also known as an independent ethics committee] review is generally required only for egg, sperm, or cell donation, or when the donors for stem cell lines are identifiable. If a public policy decision was made to recognize that human embryos have intermediate moral status requiring special respect, further guidelines and regulation would be appropriate. (To avoid misunderstanding, I do not myself believe that human embryos have significant intermediate moral status; the discussion above aims to show that even if one does believe they have significant intermediate moral status, that is not incompatible with their use and destruction in the creation of stem cell lines.)

We can conclude then that even if human embryos have intermediate moral status requiring special respect, that need not be incompatible with using and destroying them for medical research that has reasonable promise to understand, treat, or prevent serious human disease and suffering. The quotation from the president's council, however, speaks of the creation, use, and destruction of human embryos, not just the use and destruction, and that takes us directly to my focus in this [viewpoint]—the creation of embryos solely for the purpose of their use and destruction in stem cell research.

Creation of Embryos Solely for Their Use and Destruction in Stem Cell Research

I have assumed that human embryos are not full moral persons, and have just argued that their use and destruction in important stem cell research is compatible with the respect required by their possible intermediate moral status. Does the argument change if we add their *creation* for this purpose—is that now incompatible with such intermediate moral status or otherwise wrong? Before addressing this question, consider first the typical source of embryos used for stem cell research at this time, excess embryos left over from IVF undertaken for reproductive purposes. Many people believe that their use is morally permissible, and the new Obama policy permits federal funding of research using them, whereas creation of embryos solely of hESC research is not. If there is this great moral significance to these different sources of embryos, then the new Obama policy is likely correct in restricting federal funding to research embryos left over from IVF undertaken for reproductive purposes.

There is variation among reproductive clinics and patients in how many embryos will be implanted at one time in order to achieve a pregnancy, and it is typical in this country for fertility clinics to fertilize a number of eggs for potential use in IVF since it is unclear at the outset how many will be needed in order to achieve a successful pregnancy. As a result, there are many excess embryos no longer needed for further reproductive use by the couples from whose reproductive materials they were derived; these are now typically stored in freezers in IVF clinics, and it has been estimated that there are now about 400,000 such embryos in the United States. If they are not donated to others for reproductive use, these embryos will either remain frozen indefinitely or be eventually destroyed, and so will never be implanted in a uterus and allowed to develop into a human being. Some countries have legal limits to the time such embryos may be stored before being destroyed. Thus, many people believe there is nothing lost by this use since these embryos will never be implanted and allowed to develop even if not used for hESC research, while something valuable is gained by moving forward this very promising and important scientific research. If one holds that human embryos are neither human persons nor beings deserving of respect that is incompatible with their destruction, then this reasoning seems to provide strong support for favoring use of surplus embryos for hESC research. There is no serious moral objection to their use and destruction and great potential gain for human well-being from the research that made possible.

But should those who hold that embryos are either full human persons, or at least beings deserving of respect that is incompatible with their destruction, accept that a "nothing is lost principle" justifies their use and destruction for research? If the answer is yes, then this is likely to be a morally preferable source of embryos for hESC research in comparison with the creation of embryos solely for use and destruction in research. A "nothing is lost" principle seems not apply to embryos created solely for use and destruction in research since these embryos need not have been created for research in the first place. Spare embryos left over from IVF undertaken for reproductive purposes, on the other hand, will exist independent of any possible research use of them. So the idea here is that their creation for reproductive purposes was justified, but now they are not needed for reproduction, so why let them go to waste. But this line of reasoning clearly does not apply to embryos created solely for research use.

The "nothing is lost" principle, however, does not in fact justify this use of spare embryos. There are stronger and weaker versions of a "nothing is lost principle," and only the weaker and indefensible version applies to surplus embryos from IVF. Very roughly, the stronger version implies that it could be permissible to kill a person who will die very soon anyway no matter what anyone does if doing so is the only way to produce a very great good, such as saving other lives, as stem cell research might at least indirectly do. Since such a person will be dead very soon in any case, nothing is lost in the sense of significant life for that person. While admittedly controversial, the ethical intuition at work here is that since the person will inevitably die very soon even if not killed, nothing significant is lost by doing so, whereas great benefits for others can be realized. However, these surplus embryos from IVF will *not* inevitably die or be destroyed no matter what anyone does. Quite to the contrary, they will only be destroyed if someone makes the *decision* to destroy them and then does so. Otherwise, they will remain alive and frozen indefinitely, retaining at least some biological potential to develop into human beings if implanted; this potential is reduced over time during storage. So the stronger and more plausible version of the "nothing is lost" principle does not apply to them, and does not justify their destruction.

The weaker version of the "nothing is lost" principle would support the use of spare embryos in hESC research, but it is not a defensible moral principle. It looks to what will happen to the embryos given what others will *in fact* do, not given what anyone *could* do, and from that perspective nothing is lost because these embryos will in fact either be destroyed or remain frozen, and so will never be allowed to be implanted and to develop. The stronger version of the nothing is lost principle looks to whether the embryo retains the biological potential to develop, whereas the weaker version looks to whether ... it will in fact be implanted and allowed to develop into a person. Those who believe that embryos are persons or deserve respect that is incompatible with destroying them should not accept that the weaker version of the nothing is lost principle justifies the destruction of surplus embryos in hESC research. Doing so would be analogous to using an abandoned baby for research that would kill it, because if one did not [find it] it would die anyway. But the alternative for the abandoned baby, of course, is to care for it so that it does not die; it retains the biological capacity to live if given appropriate care. Those who rightly reject this weaker version of the nothing is lost principle will argue that likewise, the alternative to destroying spare embryos in hESC research is to keep them alive and frozen or to give them to others for implantation.

The weaker version of the nothing is lost principle is morally indefensible, and the stronger version, although perhaps morally defensible, does not apply to surplus embryos left over from IVF undertaken for reproductive purposes. I emphasize that the plausible version of the nothing is lost principle fails to justify the use of surplus embryos for hESC research only on the assumption that embryos are human persons or beings deserving of respect that is incompatible with their destruction, an assumption I make here but do not myself accept. So the current typical source of human embryos for hESC research is not as morally unproblematic as is often supposed and may not be any less morally problematic than the use of IVF to create embryos specifically for research and in the absence of any reproductive intent. The new Obama policy that gives substantial importance to this difference in the source of embryos may not rest on an important moral difference. As a practical matter, it is worth adding that many stem cell researchers are encountering great difficulty in obtaining enough surplus embryos left over from IVF undertaken with reproductive intent to meet their research needs, even in the absence of federal funding. . . .

Potentiality

What is the moral significance of the fact that human embryos do have the potential to be implanted, to develop, and to eventually become persons? (It is worth noting that most fertilized embryos die before they successfully complete fetal development and are born.) Does this potential give them an interest in realizing that potential, which would be clearly incompatible with their being destroyed in hESC research? Human persons, such as the embryo's potential mother and father, certainly can and typically do have a strong interest in the embryo developing into a person, but . . . I do not believe the embryo has such an interest. Likewise, an acorn has the potential under the right conditions to develop into an oak tree, but it does not have an interest in developing into an oak tree; it is indifferent to the acorn whether it does so because everything is indifferent to the acorn. The acorn is incapable of caring about whether it realizes its potential; likewise for the embryo.

If we assume, as I have here, that a human embryo is not a person with full moral status, or a being with intermediate moral status incompatible with its destruction, then it is either a possible or potential person because of its potential. Does having that potential give it a right to be born, or a right to realize that potential? I think the answer must be no. There are an infinite number of possible persons, all the persons that might come into existence as the result of the fertilization of a specific egg by a specific sperm. No one of those possible persons has a right to come into existence as a person; indeed, since possible persons do not exist and are not organisms or entities at all, it is unclear how they could be the bearers of rights at all. Under the above assumptions, I think we should say the same about potential persons, the case of already existing embryos. If they cannot have an interest in becoming a person because they do not have any interests at all, then they cannot have a right to become a person and realize their potential.

Again, it might be objected that embryos certainly do have interests—they have an interest in all the conditions necessary for them to remain alive. Likewise, one might hold that other living things like plants have an interest in conditions like water and sunlight necessary for them to remain alive and to develop. But this would be a mistake. We need to distinguish whether either the embryo or plant has an interest in remaining alive from the conditions necessary for them to remain alive. They would have an interest in the latter conditions only if they had the former interest in remaining alive. But I have already argued that as a being lacking sentience or consciousness, the embryo (and likewise a plant) does not have interests or a good of its own, and therefore no specific interest in remaining alive. Of course, the woman and man who created it will typically have a very strong interest in it remaining alive, and this gives them a derivative interest in the embryo obtaining the conditions necessary to do so. The same would be true of a plant that they valued—they would have an interest in the plant getting water and sunlight. But in each case, these would be their interests, not the interests of the embryo or plant itself.

Potential is clearly relevant to the economic value of a thing—if a young pony has the potential to develop into a horse that can run faster than any other horse, its economic value as a racehorse is much greater than another pony that lacks that potential. Likewise, potential is relevant to the instrumental value of something in achieving a desired end. Organs that can be used for transplantation have more instrumental value than organs that are unusable for transplantation. The economic and instrumental value of an entity or thing is the value it has for some purpose or for others, not its intrinsic value. The relevant question for potential's impact on the moral status of an embryo is whether the fact that an embryo has the potential to develop into a human person, even though while still an embryo it is not a human person, is sufficient to confer on the embryo the moral status it will later have after it becomes a human person. If Sarah who has a terminal illness writes her will leaving her house to her daughter, then her daughter is potentially the inheritor of the house with the right as inheritor then to sell the house to others. But until she is the inheritor, not just potentially the inheritor, she has no right to sell the house. If Sam has the potential to run faster than all the other competitors in the race, then he has the potential to claim the prize, but he has no actual claim or right to the prize until this potential becomes actuality and he has in fact run faster than all the other competitors. Moral rights in general have this character—they are grounded in the actual, not just potential, properties of a being. So the embryo's potential to become a person is relevant to the moral status it will have if and when it does become a person, but it does not confer the moral status on it when still an embryo that it will have later when it has become a person.

In the case of embryos produced by cloning or SCNT, some scientists believe these human embryos would have little if any potential or probability of developing to the point that they could be born alive, certainly born alive and healthy. That is consistent with experience attempting to clone some animals whose developmental complexity and demands are much less than those of humans. If these scientists are correct, then it would be a mistake to ascribe to cloned human embryos even any significant potential to become a born human person, whatever the moral significance of such potential might be if they had it. And if cloned human embryos lack any significant potential to develop and be born alive, then the putative slippery slope from research to reproductive cloning feared by many opponents of the latter is not slippery at all; the former cannot lead to the latter.

Cloning Is Morally Permissible

So if it is permissible to use embryos in research in the course of which it is known that they will be destroyed, why should it not be permissible as well to create them for that purpose by means that are not intrinsically immoral? People who believe that it is permissible to use and destroy animals in research typically also accept the creation or breeding of animals for that use. If the potential value of the hESC research in which embryos are used and destroyed together with the nature of embryos at the blastocyst stage makes their use and destruction in research morally permissible, then why should creating embryos for this permissible use not also be permissible? No one believes that the creation of a human embryo is in itself morally wrong and impermissible, and most do not believe that doing so by artificial means such as IVF is either. These are either morally neutral or good actions, not morally wrong or bad. But I have argued earlier as well that the use of human embryos in hESC research that will result in their destruction is also morally permissible, and indeed morally good given the promise of that research. So if neither the creation of the embryo, nor its use and destruction in hESC research, is bad or impermissible, how could it be that the combination of the two somehow becomes bad or impermissible?

Much of what I have argued above applies equally to the creation of embryos by SCNT if and when that becomes possible. Few people believe that cloning in itself is wrong, and it is hard to see what the basis of such a view might be. If mice or genes are cloned for research, doing so is rarely opposed. It is the use of cloning to produce human beings that is widely opposed—human reproductive cloning. I have argued elsewhere that the arguments against human reproductive cloning are a good deal less compelling than is widely believed. But in the context of SCNT to create embryos for research, reproductive cloning is not at issue. Some have asserted that there might be a "slippery slope" between research and reproductive cloning, such that perfecting the former makes the latter more likely. But as I noted above, as a matter of biological science that may not be the case, and in any event reproductive cloning can be prohibited without prohibiting research cloning. So why should cloning of embryos for use in hESC research be any more morally problematic than the creation of embryos by IVF for research? So far as I can see it is not.

> "Embryos are embryos regardless of how they were made, and thus cloning is cloning, whatever the purpose."

Research Cloning Is Not Ethical

William Saunders, Michael Fragoso, and David Prentice

In the following viewpoint, William Saunders, Michael Fragoso, and David Prentice from the Family Research Council (www.frc.org) contend that human cloning is wrong, regardless of whether it is done for research or reproductive purposes. The authors discuss cloning initiatives in California and Missouri that they say are based on false claims of ethical cloning. The proponents of these initiatives, say Saunders, Fragoso, and Prentice, are trying to mislead the public by maintaining that cloning for reproduction and cloning for research are two different acts. In reality, the authors say, both types of cloning involve the same experimental process, and the only difference between the two is the reason or motivation behind doing them. According to Saunders, Fragoso, and Prentice, there is no such thing as ethical cloning. William Saunders and David Prentice are fellows, and

Michael Fragoso is a research assistant, at the Family Research Council, a conservative Christian group that advocates for traditional family values.

As you read, consider the following questions:

1. What was the final vote on Missouri's Amendment 2, according to the authors?

2. According to the viewpoint, people who make the argument that cloning is cloning whatever the purpose are written off by William Neaves as what?

3. According to the authors, Missouri's constitution says that if an individual clones a person it is a crime to try to implant the clone in a uterus. Thus, they say, the Missouri constitution forbids an entire class of people from doing what?

In recent years, a growing number of state governments have embarked on cloning initiatives, often linked to efforts to promote human embryonic stem cell research. Legislation has ranged from protecting certain kinds of human cloning and embryonic stem cell research (i.e., ensuring they cannot be "outlawed"), to funding the practices directly. One can only expect that, given the inflated media coverage, this trend will continue.

The best known of these initiatives were in California and Missouri. Each amended the state constitution, rather than state laws, making repeal more difficult. California's Proposition 71 from 2004, known as the "California Stem Cell Research and Cures Initiative" ("Prop 71"), was crafted specifically to fund embryonic stem cell research and human cloning, while the 2006 Missouri Amendment 2, the "Missouri Stem Cell Research and Cures Initiative" ("Amendment 2"), enshrined the right to engage in human cloning in the Missouri state constitution.

Supporters of both measures made similar claims—that embryonic stem cell research and human cloning provide effective cures for diseases; that embryonic stem cell research and cloning would provide economic growth; and that by enshrining embryonic stem cell research and cloning in law, the state would provide meaningful ethical oversight.

Yet each one of these claims is false.

California Prop 71

Prop 71 was an initiative on the ballot for the 2004 elections. Prop 71 itself sought to achieve a number of goals: to form the California Institute for Regenerative Medicine ("CIRM"), to establish a California "constitutional right" to engage in embryonic stem cell research, to provide oversight for CIRM, and to provide almost $3 billion for CIRM through the issuance of bonds.

In the lead up to the vote, those in favor of Prop 71 raised and spent a prodigious amount of money—$25 million (versus $400,000 spent by its opposition). Prop 71 passed by a margin of 59.1 percent in favor to 40.9 percent opposed. As a result, CIRM was organized and funded through a general obligation bond issue, and the California constitution now contains Article XXXV, protecting embryonic stem cell research and human cloning.

Missouri Amendment 2

Two years later, the people of Missouri were asked to vote on their own constitutional amendment. Amendment 2 ostensibly sought to ensure "that Missouri patients have access to stem cell therapies and cures, that Missouri researchers can conduct stem cell research in the state, and that such research is conducted safely and ethically. . . ." Amendment 2 was touted as the best hope for cures for the infirm, as well as a potential engine of economic growth for Missouri, and as a much-needed source of an ethical scientific framework. It was promoted as a "cloning ban."

As in California, a significant portion of the initiative was geared towards ensuring funding for embryonic stem cell research and human cloning (called "somatic cell nuclear transfer" or "SCNT") from the state government—that is from taxpayers. Also as in California, the pro-cloning side spent exorbitant amounts of money advancing their cause—over $30 million. Nevertheless, a last minute campaign by Amendment 2's opponents, who took issue with its deceptive nature, almost succeeded in defeating it. The final vote was 51.2 percent in favor, 48.8 percent opposed. The lead had been steadily narrowing from the original 30 point advantage in favor of the initiative. Polling revealed that if the vote had come a few days later, Amendment 2 would have been defeated.

In both California and Missouri, those promoting cloning initiatives made similar claims. In all cases, those claims have proven to be at best deceptive, and at worst, false. . . .

Missouri's Amendment 2, in particular, used misleading phrasing to trick voters into thinking that they were voting for an initiative to set clear, consensus-based ethical boundaries against the practice of human cloning. In reality, Amendment 2 sought to enshrine certain human cloning procedures in the Missouri constitution.

Amendment 2 says clearly in the beginning, "No person may clone or attempt to clone a human being" (38(d)2(1)). It is not until four subsections later, when terms are defined, that we find out that "clone or attempt to clone a human being" in this law "means to implant in a uterus or attempt to implant in a uterus anything other than the product of fertilization of an egg of a human female by a sperm of a human male for the purpose of initiating a pregnancy that could result in the creation of a human fetus or the birth of a human being" (38(d)6(2)). In other words, the statute says that cloning a human being is only illegal if the clone is implanted in a uterus with the intent of allowing it to develop into a more mature human being. If it is killed before that happens, the

Definition of SCNT

[Somatic cell nuclear transfer (SCNT)—]a technique that combines an enucleated egg [one having had the nucleus removed] and the nucleus of a somatic cell [any body cell other than an egg or sperm] to make an embryo. SCNT can be used for therapeutic or reproductive purposes, but the initial stage that combines an enucleated egg and a somatic cell nucleus is the same.

"Glossary—Somatic Cell Nuclear Transfer,"
US National Institutes of Health, August 20, 2010.
http://stemcells.nih.gov.

law would allow it. However, "implantation" does not change what the embryo is—it is a living human being from day one. The law was dishonest as to the very meaning of the practice it claimed to forbid!

Cloning Is Cloning Is Cloning

SCNT is the process by which someone or something is cloned. It is the same procedure that gave us Dolly the sheep. It really is the definition of cloning, i.e., removing the nucleus of an "egg" (or, oocyte) and replacing it with the nucleus from an ordinary body (or "somatic") cell; this is *somatic cell nuclear transfer* or SCNT.

The proponents of Amendment 2 played a semantic game, changing the definition of cloning from the creation of a genetically identical human being to the creation (and *implantation*) of a genetically identical human being *for reproductive purposes*. Thus the Missouri "cloning *ban*" does no such thing; it merely bans a specific *motivation* for cloning. If you want to create it to kill it, that's okay. If you want to create it to bring it to birth, that isn't. As one newspaper put it following the passage of this deceptive initiative, "a clone by any other name, such as 'somatic cell nuclear transfer,' is still a clone."

The proponents, however, could not disagree more. William Neaves, president and CEO of the Stowers Institute for Medical Research, insists to this day that, "It does not represent a newly conceived life. It has been cultured in a lab dish from an ordinary body cell of an already-living person conceived years ago." This statement is a mixture of technical truths that actually implies a falsehood. A cloned embryo is not, in fact, "conceived" as conception is normally understood, that is, as involving normal, sexual reproduction. It *is* created, in a "lab dish" from a "body cell," in a sense, as noted above. But none of this is germane to what *it* is: namely a new, living *human being*.

Neaves has made such declarations in the past. "When people hear the phrase 'clone a human being' they think of an attempt to make a human version of Dolly the sheep. No one thinks of making a few dozen cells in a Petri dish," Neaves told the *Washington Post*. However, if people think that the sort of cloning Neaves advocates is "an attempt to make a human version of Dolly the sheep," they are absolutely *right*. Dolly the sheep was created *by the same process of SCNT* that was legalized in Missouri. Dolly the sheep was at first a *sheep* embryo, *just as the embryos* Neaves wants to use for stem cell research are *human* embryos.

People who make the scientific argument that embryos are embryos regardless of how they were made, and thus cloning is cloning, whatever the purpose, are written off by Neaves as religious fundamentalists. He says that basing public policy on the facts of cloning "would be comparable to outlawing blood transfusions because some Christians believe it's wrong." Scientific observations with which he disagrees become "beliefs."

Neaves's California counterpart, Larry Goldstein, once said of pro-lifers, "Another downside is that some opponents of embryonic stem cell research speak about this research in terms of Nazi-type experiments, or violating the civil rights of embryos, or murdering blastocysts. They often make outrageous and totally distorted scientific claims because they don't actually understand the science. I feel bad about the implications that I'm a murderer when I'm driven actually by trying to do something good and trying to educate the public. It's difficult when opponents feel no compunction about scientific distortions and falsehoods." However, Goldstein's statements merely confuse the issues.

That embryo-destructive research kills blastocysts (which are humans in a predictable stage of embryonic development) is indisputable scientifically. Whether blastocysts are "murdered" in "Nazi-type experiments" or embryos "have their civil rights violated" is a *philosophical* question about the dignity and inviolability of innocent human life, on which proponents and opponents of human cloning disagree. Yet Goldstein describes this *moral* disagreement as "outrageous and totally distorted *scientific* claims" (Emphasis added). However, the science is indisputable—embryo destruction kills blastocysts. Goldstein confuses his categories by referring to the *moral consequences* of the science *as the science itself.* Goldstein dismisses his opponents' science as mere ideology, while Neaves simply dismisses his opponents themselves as religious fundamentalists.

Ironically, in many ways it's Neaves's "scientific" arguments that are exercises in post-modern philosophy: Scientific facts ("what is cloning?") can be changed by the names we give them. This is an argument articulated prior to Neaves's advocacy in the journal *Science* in 2002. In it, the authors argue that while SCNT might be used both "to create a genetically identical copy of a biological entity," and for "making stem cells for regenerative medicine," these two "goals" are "substantially different." In fact, the authors assert "the distinction between the objectives of these two very different lines of investigation" requires new language to be adopted. SCNT for the sake of creating "a genetically identical copy" is "cloning," whereas SCNT for the sake of stem cells ought to be called "nuclear transplantation." The authors ignore the fact that, regardless of why SCNT takes place, its invariable effect is "to create a genetically identical copy of a biological entity." It is from that entity that the embryonic stem cells are extracted. In spite of what the authors say about how differing motivations alter the nature of the procedure, the procedure is "cloning" in both cases *by their own definition.*

Cloning Is a Scientific Act, Not a Motive

Sadly, the Missouri constitution adopted this view that what makes a clone is motivation, not science. As such, it says that if you clone a person, it is a crime to try to implant it in a uterus so as to allow it to mature. Thus, there is an entire class of people (those created by human cloning) that the Missouri constitution forbids from following their natural biological development, seemingly relegating them to being used in scientific experimentation.

If a state really wants to ban cloning, it must ban the intentional creation of genetically identical human beings at any stage—regardless of purpose. In fact, a grassroots organization in Missouri, Cures Without Cloning, is trying to do just that in the wake of Amendment 2. In their own ballot initiative, seeking to amend the Missouri constitution, Cures Without Cloning proposes defining cloning by saying,

> For all purposes within this article, "Clone or attempt to clone a human being" means create or attempt to create a human embryo at any stage, which shall include the one-cell stage onward, by any means other than fertilization of a human egg by a human sperm.

This definition attempts to ban the *act* of cloning, unlike the current law which simply bans a motivation for doing so.

Nevertheless, Cures Without Cloning faced more of the same semantic distortions from the pro-cloning forces in Missouri. On October 11, 2007, Robin Carnahan, Missouri's secretary of state, issued the official ballot summary for the anti-cloning initiative saying that it seeks "to repeal the current ban on human cloning or attempted cloning and to limit Missouri patients' access to stem cell research, therapies and cures approved by voters in November 2006." In other words, expanding a partial cloning ban to cover *all* cloning is, according to her, a *repeal* of a cloning ban. By Carnahan's logic, more is less and less is more.

The *St. Louis Post-Dispatch* said, in defense of Carnahan, that pro-life activists want to prohibit stem cell research and preserve "microscopic dividing cells in a Petri dish." This, as we have shown above, simply dehumanizes the embryo by a linguistic trick.

In response to this double-talk from both Carnahan and the media, a lawsuit was brought by Cures Without Cloning alleging bias in the ballot summary. On February 20, Cole County circuit judge Patricia Joyce ruled that the existing ballot language was "insufficient and unfair." The description was changed to say the purpose of the initiative is "prohibiting human cloning that is conducted by creating a human embryo at any stage from the one-cell stage forward; prohibiting expenditure of taxpayer dollars on research or experimentation on human cloning; and allowing stem cell research for therapies and cures that complies with these prohibitions and the prohibitions of Section 38(d) of the Constitution."

Regrettably, the state court of appeals overturned this decision, changing the language to read that the initiative would "change the current ban"—rather than Carnahan's preferred "repeal the current ban." The decision came so late in the political process that it prevented Missouri pro-life groups from putting the initiative on the November 2008 ballot, which is precisely what the pro-cloners wanted.

In the future, many states will be tempted to pass constitutional amendments similar to California's Prop 71 and Missouri's Amendment 2. They will be attracted to human cloning and embryonic stem cell research by the same siren songs of miracle cures, expanded revenue, and ethical benchmarks. As we have seen, all of these claims are overstated. The cures are not forthcoming. The revenue is purely hypothetical. The ethics are mere doublespeak. We hope that . . . the reader [of this viewpoint] will be ready to refute these claims when they are made in his or her state.

| "Induced pluripotent stem cells have all the potential of embryonic stem cells without ending any human lives."

Induced Pluripotent Stem Cell Research Is Morally Superior to Research Cloning

Right to Life of Michigan Education Fund

In the following viewpoint, Right to Life of Michigan Education Fund contends that induced pluripotent stem cell (iPSC) research provides an ethical way to advance medical treatments. The author says that iPSC research can produce pluripotent stem cells that won't trigger an immune response in patients receiving treatments, initiatives that scientists thought only embryonic stem cells and cloning could provide. Thus, says the author, iPSC research eliminates the need to clone and destroy human embryos in harvesting embryonic stem cells. Right to Life of Michigan Education Fund is a pro-life organization dedicated to protecting life from fertilization to natural death.

As you read, consider the following questions:

1. Why can the term "adult" in adult stem cells be misleading, according to the author?

2. According to the viewpoint, discoveries of ways to make adult human skin cells mimic embryonic stem cells occurred at which two universities?

3. The author says that medical science must be about protecting human life, not ending it. What examples of medical science that did not protect human life does the author provide?

Proponents of human embryonic stem cell research often cite all of the potential treatments that may result from the research but fail to mention that human life is destroyed when removing these cells from a human embryo. Now researchers have pioneered a different kind of treatment that carries the same potential for treating disease . . . without destroying human lives.

Recent advances in research have found a way to potentially duplicate all the promises of embryonic stem cell research without endangering human life. There are two basic kinds of stem cells: embryonic and adult.

What is embryonic stem cell research? This research involves taking the stem cells out of embryos, which results in the destruction of the embryo. These stem cells, in embryos only several days old, are the foundation cells that will produce the more than 200 kinds of tissue in a human body. The potential that embryonic stem cells have is the ability to produce any type of tissue (pluripotency).

What is adult stem cell research? This research involves using stem cells from adult patients. The term "adult" can be misleading, because these cells are found in many places like baby teeth and umbilical cord blood, none of which involves harming human life. These cells are already programmed to

No Need to Pursue Research Cloning

Studies of pluripotent human stem cells will undoubtedly advance our understanding of human biology. Patients may someday benefit from new therapies based on stem cell research. These are noble purposes. Yet do we really need to continue research on pluripotent stem cells derived from human embryos when we can obtain cells with the same properties in an ethically uncompromised way? Do we need to pursue human cloning as a means of generating patient-specific stem cells when we can produce them so readily from adult skin?

Maureen L. Condic,
"Getting Stem Cells Right,"
First Things, *February 2008.*

repair specific damaged tissue in the body. Although it might not make national news, embryonic stem cells haven't treated any diseases in humans yet. Adult stem cell treatments, however, are being created and used for more than 70 conditions.

Why the focus on human embryonic stem cells? While embryonic stem cells have yet to treat anybody, some researchers state that embryonic stem cells have more potential than adult stem cells. Even though there are many problems with embryonic stem cells, like uncontrollable tumor growth and patients' immune rejection concerns, researchers continue to rebel against any restrictions or regulations addressing the research.

Recent advances have found a way around using embryonic stem cells. In November of 2007, researchers from Kyoto University and the University of Wisconsin independently discovered ways to make adult human skin cells mimic embryonic stem cells. Preliminary tests show these cells (induced pluripotent stem cells, or iPSC for short) have the same ability to turn into any type of tissue in the body.

iPSC research avoids ethical dilemmas and practical problems with embryonic stem cells; ends cloning. Induced pluripotent stem cells have all the potential of embryonic stem cells without ending any human lives. These advances can also fix two key problems with embryonic stem cells. If a patient's own skin cells can be used to treat her, her body's immune system won't reject what is already a part of her. Also, it takes many destroyed embryos to produce a large amount of stem cells. To find enough embryos, researchers have proposed cloning humans (also called therapeutic cloning or somatic cell nuclear transfer). Patients' skin cells are numerous and could be used to "cure themselves."

Many people have ethical objections to destroying human embryos. Many people have legitimate concerns with the destruction of human life for human embryonic stem cell treatments. A poll of 500 Michigan voters in 2007 showed that 70 percent do not support stem cell research that kills human embryos. In 2006, Missouri passed a misleading constitutional amendment by less than 51 percent. The amendment was promoted as banning human cloning but actually allows constitutionally protected cloning of humans for embryonic stem cell research.

Medical science must be about protecting human life, not ending it. Did Nazi medical experiments on concentration camp prisoners and human syphilis testing on African-Americans in Tuskegee, Alabama, advance the human condition? We can advance medical treatments with stem cells without destroying human life.

"The only way critics can have no moral problem with the new [induced pluripotent stem cell] research is if their concern about cloning is not, in fact, about the destruction of potential life."

Research Cloning and Induced Pluripotent Stem Cell Research Are Morally Equivalent

Gregory E. Kaebnick

In the following viewpoint, philosopher Gregory E. Kaebnick contends that induced pluripotent stem cell (iPSC) research is not without moral concerns. In iPSC research, genes inserted into an adult skin cell reprogram the cell to act like an embryo. According to Kaebnick, this is very similar to somatic cell nuclear transfer, or cloning, where the nucleus of an adult skin cell is replaced with the nucleus of a different body cell. In both cases, says Kaebnick, something akin to an embryo is created. He says that if those who oppose embryonic stem cell research and cloning are against it because of the potential destruction of human life, they should have a moral problem with iPSC research as

Gregory E. Kaebnick, "Embryonic Ethics," thehastingscenter.org/bioethicsforum, January 25, 2008. Copyright © 2008 by Hastings Center Report. All rights reserved. Reproduced by permission.

well. Gregory E. Kaebnick is the editor of the Hastings Center Report, *the bimonthly journal of the Hastings Center, an independent bioethics research institute.*

As you read, consider the following questions:

1. According to Kaebnick, what did a member of the President's Council on Bioethics suggest that the "thing" that is produced from somatic cell nuclear transfer be called in order to distinguish it from a zygote?

2. According to Kaebnick, what did researchers involved in iPSC research call the balls that formed from stem cell lines?

3. What does Kaebnick say is a common concern among the debates about genetic enhancement of children, sports doping, genetic modification of livestock, extirpation of endangered species, and commercial development of places "untrammeled by man"?

There is another side to the blockbuster announcement last year [2007] that researchers have learned how to create stem cells by genetically reprogramming skin cells, turning back their developmental clock so that they acquire the capacity to become almost any type of cell in the body. The news was hailed as sweeping aside the moral objections to research on embryonic stem cells. It also showed that those objections were not what we thought they were.

Just Another Kind of Embryo

First, it's important to see that the new procedure might turn out to be analogous to somatic cell nuclear transfer [SCNT], commonly just called cloning. In SCNT, researchers remove the nucleus from an egg and insert the nucleus of a fully differentiated cell from the body—often a skin cell. The egg's cytoplasm then reprograms the nucleus, resulting in what seems to qualify as a new kind of human embryo. To be sure, the new thing differs from the standard kind of embryo in some ways: no sperm is required, and no sexual recombination of genes occurs. For some, this difference has seemed significant enough to warrant a difference in classification; Paul McHugh, a member of the President's Council on Bioethics, wrote in 2004 that SCNT looked more like tissue culture than reproduction, and he suggested that the thing created through SCNT be called a "clonote" to distinguish it from a zygote, the first step in embryonic development.

But there are lumpers and splitters when it comes to scientific classifications, and the lumpers seem to have won out. SCNT still involves eggs, and the resulting entity looks much like a zygote and may well be capable of developing into a baby. At any rate, the process has worked reasonably well for some other species, and as the science advances, it will probably eventually work for humans.

Cloning is now the *traditional procedure,* odd as that sounds, for reprogramming a cell. In the new technique, a cell can be reprogrammed without the help of the egg's cytoplasm, just by inserting some new genes. The resulting cells do not look much like embryos, but they can turn into all of the major tissue types of the body and presumably could differentiate into every kind of cell needed to create a person.

No one is yet calling these new entities "embryos." Possibly a reprogrammed skin cell lacks the capacity to develop the extra-embryonic tissues, such as a placenta, that it would need in order to implant and come to term. Certainly it looks different; it lacks the egg's massive cytoplasm. Yet it is too early to say definitively that the new entities are not embryos. If reprogramming through cloning creates a new sort of embryo, different from natural human embryos in important ways, then this new kind of reprogramming might prove to be creating *yet another* new kind of embryo. Traditional cloning shows that sperm are not needed to create an embryo. There may be nothing magical about the egg, either. In principle, an embryo could be created entirely from scratch.

Of course, whether scientists can create embryos from skin cells is a testable proposition. In the research recently announced, some cell lines formed balls that the researchers called "embryoid." For all we now know, as the science advances, forthcoming research might produce balls that are "embryoid" not only in appearance but also in how they can develop.

But the critics of embryonic stem cell research are unconcerned. Richard Doerflinger, who works at the U.S. Conference of Catholic Bishops and is a leading opponent of embryonic stem cell research, has said of the new research that he sees "no moral problem with it at all." This is its own blockbuster development. The objection they have lodged against embryonic stem cell research is that it would require the destruction of embryos, which is murder. A reprogrammed skin cell is certainly not the usual kind of embryo, but destroying one may still turn out to be tantamount to the destruction of potential life, and so to count as murder. The only way critics can have no moral problem with the new research is if their concern about cloning is not, in fact, about the destruction of potential life.

Altering Natural Affairs

But then what is the objection? One possibility is that even though an egg is not needed to create an embryo, the egg itself is morally significant. Here's the idea that might be at work: A skin cell can be tweaked so that it acquires the potential to become a person, but that potential is artificial and morally unimportant—a product of the laboratory that may also be taken away in the laboratory. The moral identity of a reprogrammed skin cell is still just "skin cell," not "embryo." We can buy it and sell it, culture it and destroy it, and no one really cares.

Induced Pluripotent Stem Cell Research Does Not End the Debate

The use of human iPS [induced pluripotent stem] cells is significantly less ethically problematic than the use of human ES [embryonic stem] cells, not least of which is that the production of iPS cells does not require any direct harm to embryos and thereby largely avoids the main source of controversy in the stem cell debate. However, human iPS cells are unlikely to end the stem cell debate since they are generated through knowledge based on human ES cells, which will continue to be needed for the foreseeable future as "gold standard" PS cells. Moreover, the use of iPS cells raises ethical concerns specific to somatic cell reprogramming, although in many instances we can reasonably expect current problems to be overcome in the proximate future. Thus, while the use of human iPS cells will do much to mitigate the stem cell debate, the controversy will most certainly survive.

Julia C. Watt and Nao R. Kobayashi,
"The Bioethics of Human Pluripotent Stem Cells:
Will Induced Pluripotent Stem Cells End the Debate?,"
Open Stem Cell Journal, *2010.*

On the other hand, eggs and the embryos produced from them are *expected* to try to become people. Their potential is natural, not artificial. Further, because eggs and embryos are morally special—witness the concerns people often have about selling them—intervening in their natural development is morally troubling.

This picture makes the objection to cloning comparable to concerns that arise in a range of other debates about what we can do in and to nature—genetic enhancement of children, sports doping, genetic modification of livestock, extirpation of endangered species, and commercial development of places "untrammeled by man," as the Wilderness Act puts it.

These debates have many differences, but they all feature a common concern about alteration of natural affairs and processes.

If this is right, then we need to rethink the debate over traditional cloning. The moral concerns about taking human life are powerful and clear and lead directly to public policy that upholds those concerns. The moral concerns we might have about intervening into the natural processes of human life may still be very deeply felt, but they are extremely complicated and may not lead neatly to public policy.

> *"It seems absurd to require that women who want to support embryo research should be required to be more altruistic than those who give their eggs for reproductive purposes."*

It Is Ethical to Pay Women to Donate Eggs for Research Cloning

Bonnie Steinbock

In the following viewpoint, philosopher Bonnie Steinbock argues that women who donate oocytes (egg cells) for research purposes deserve to be compensated for their time and trouble. Steinbock can see no reason or justification for policies that allow women to be compensated when they donate eggs for reproductive purposes but deny it when the eggs are donated for research. Bonnie Steinbock is a professor of philosophy at the State University of New York (SUNY) at Albany and a specialist in bioethics.

As you read, consider the following questions:

1. According to Steinbock, which state is believed to be the first state to allow payment to women who provide eggs for research?

2. According Steinbock, how much can women who donate their eggs earn?

3. According to Steinbock, what did the ethics board point out about the social value of embryonic stem cell research, i.e., research requiring egg cells, and that of enabling individuals to reproduce?

On June 11, [New York's] Empire State Stem Cell Board voted to allow funding of research on stem cell lines derived using eggs donated solely for research purposes, where the donor was compensated for her expense, time, burden, and discomfort, within specified limits, as is currently permitted when women donate oocytes [eggs] for reproductive purposes in New York State. Although the wording of the resolution focused on the funding of research, in effect it allows women who donate oocytes for research purposes to be paid. New York is believed to be the first state to allow payment to women who provide eggs for research.

Objections Seem Political

Why have other states, which allow compensation to women who donate their eggs for reproductive purposes, declined to permit such compensation if the oocytes will be used in research? Clearly, there is a political rationale.

Given that embryonic stem cell research is very controversial, supporters have attempted to avoid charges of "commercialization" and "commodification" by taking payment to egg donors off the table. Politics aside, are there good reasons against compensating egg providers if the eggs will be used for research?

One objection comes from Alan O. Trounson, president of the California Institute for Regenerative Medicine, who told the *Chronicle of Higher Education* that stem cell researchers need large numbers of eggs only if they plan to create embryonic stem cells through somatic cell nuclear transfer, or cloning. Some scientists are exploring less controversial ways of deriving stem cells, such as induced pluripotent stem cells, or iPS cells.

According to Trounson, reviewers for the institute "have not supported any recent applications for nuclear transfer in the human but are supporting many iPS cell studies." He added that leading scientists think that iPS cells offer something more than nuclear transfer at present.

However, even if cloning human embryos does not prove fruitful as a source of stem cells, human oocytes might have other uses in research. As George Daley, a stem cell researcher at Harvard and Children's Hospital Boston, points out in the *New York Times*, "There are many questions you can only answer by studying human eggs."

Moreover, the objection does not address the ethics of payment at all. If oocytes are not needed for research, then women will not be encouraged to donate. The payment question is whether they should be compensated if they do donate. Is there a reason to treat differently donors whose eggs will be used for reproduction and donors whose eggs will be used for research?

One concern is exploitation of women who might be induced to donate by the prospect of earning as much as $10,000 per cycle. "It will be the vulnerable classes of cash-strapped and college-aged women who will be exploited by the state in this scheme," said Rev. Thomas V. Berg, a member of the state stem cell board's ethics committee who is also a Roman Catholic priest.

Undue inducement is a real concern in egg donation generally. For many women, the chance to earn $5,000 to $10,000 would be very attractive, and might lead them to discount the burdens (two weeks of daily injections and what has been characterized as comparable to "the worst period you've ever had") and risks.

Women Are Always Asked to Be Altruistic

For all the lip service paid to altruism regarding egg donation, and regarding reproductive technology more generally, we do not question that doctors should be paid for helping create and transfer embryos or that the nurses assisting them should receive compensation for their time and energy, nor do we question that the lawyers who draw up the donating contracts should be paid. Instead, it is only the payment offered to egg donors that causes such consternation and concern. As [researcher] Lori Andrews (1992) points out, "[I]n most instances, when society suggests that a certain activity should be done for altruism, rather than money, it is generally a woman's activity". If we are going to allow gamete [reproductive cell, i.e., egg or sperm cell] transfer in the United States, women should be well paid for it, because it is time-consuming, uncomfortable, risky, and potentially life-threatening.

Anna Curtis, "Giving 'Til It Hurts: Egg Donation and the Costs of Altruism," Feminist Formations, Summer 2010.

However, the burdens and risks are precisely the same, regardless of how the eggs are used. The potential for exploitation does not justify treating donors differently. Moreover, women who are given full information about the risks and burdens are surely capable of making the decision to donate for themselves.

If the exploitation objection errs on the side of overprotecting women, and thus veers on paternalism, a different concern is that women should be motivated by altruism, not money. But why should egg providers be motivated solely by altruism?

Women Who Donate Eggs for Research Should Not Be Treated Differently

Everyone involved in infertility treatment gets paid: the doctors, the nurses, the receptionists—why should those who provide the eggs be the only ones who are expected to give of their time, and undergo risks and burdens, for free? Justice requires reasonable compensation for the time, expense, burden and discomfort occasioned by the procedure.

It is accepted practice for women to provide eggs to other women who want to have babies. Surely the same consideration applies in the case of eggs for research, since the time, expense, burdens, and risks are identical. Although women who provide eggs to other women who want to have babies typically do have altruistic motives, virtually no women are willing to undergo the rigors of egg donation to strangers without some compensation.

It seems absurd to require that women who want to support embryo research (without which, it should be noted, infertility treatment would not exist, and cannot further progress) should be required to be more altruistic than those who give their eggs for reproductive purposes. Moreover, as the ethics board pointed out, the social value of the research is potentially greater than that of enabling individuals to reproduce.

The argument made by the board was not simply that the research requires eggs and women are being paid for their eggs anyway. It was that the research is morally permissible and potentially extremely valuable, and that similar cases should be treated alike, a fundamental principle of reason and justice.

> *"Paying women for eggs will necessarily lead to the undue inducement and consequent exploitation of women."*

It Is Not Ethical to Pay Women to Donate Eggs for Research Cloning

Thomas Berg

In the following viewpoint, Thomas Berg says New York's Empire State Stem Cell Board got it wrong when members voted to allow researchers to pay women for their eggs. Berg contends that poor women in need of money will feel compelled to donate their eggs despite the very serious health risks associated with the egg harvesting procedure. Paying women to donate their eggs will lead to their exploitation, says Berg. Thomas Berg, a Roman Catholic priest, is executive director of the Westchester Institute for Ethics and the Human Person and a member of the ethics committee of New York's Empire State Stem Cell Board.

As you read, consider the following questions:

1. In addition to allowing researchers to pay women for their eggs, Berg is shocked because New York is taking the issue further by doing what?

2. According to Berg, ovarian hyperstimulation syndrome (OHSS) can cause bloating, nausea, and what other medical problems?

3. According to Berg, egg-donation agencies have seen an increase in applicants, as high as what percentage in some places?

On May 12 [2009], my colleagues on the ethics committee of New York's Empire State Stem Cell Board voted overwhelmingly to recommend that state funds be awarded to researchers who have paid women for their "time and burden" in the retrieval of their eggs for research purposes.

If adopted by New York's full stem cell board, the measure will mimic the long-established practice in the assisted-reproduction industry of paying up to $10,000 per retrieval. New York would become the first state in the union to allow such reimbursements to eggs-for-research donors.

As if paying women indirectly for their eggs were not shocking enough, New York is anxious to take this issue further by using state monies to "reimburse" women directly for their egg donations. Several thousand taxpayer dollars would be handed over to any woman who undergoes the dangerous process of egg donation.

Such aggressive monetary reimbursements have been disallowed in most states, including California and Massachusetts, both of which are enthusiastic about stem cell research.

Even the University of Pennsylvania ethicist Arthur Caplan, a pro-cloning advocate, thinks paying women for eggs is a bad idea: "The market in eggs tries to incentivize women to do something they otherwise would not do. Egg sales and egg rebates are not the ethical way to go."

Exploitation of Women

Paying donors is wrong because egg donation entails very serious health risks for women, which can include moderate to

The Commodification of Women

Opponents of compensation [to women for their eggs] declare that permitting payment will lead to the commodification of women and of human life. In the context of egg donation for reproductive purposes and surrogacy, some feminists argue that "in this non-ideal world of ours, treating women like anonymous fungible breeders objectifies them and recreates subordination." Likewise, opponents claim that compensating women for supplying their eggs for stem cell research objectifies them by "translat[ing] women's bodies and their physiological processes into a product," thereby turning women and their reproductive material into chattel, diminishing the value of the individual generally, and violating conceptions of personhood. Paying a woman for her eggs also amounts to paying for a bodily intrusion, which similarly undermines personhood. Further, opponents assert that combining payment with donation for research purposes might create a caste system: minority women, poorer women, and women without academic or athletic achievements will become the suppliers of eggs for research while white women, economically advantaged women, and accomplished women (according to societal norms) will continue to provide eggs for reproductive purposes.

Pamela Foohey,
"Paying Women for Their Eggs for Use in Stem Cell Research,"
Pace Law Review, *Spring 2010.*

serious ovarian hyperstimulation syndrome (OHSS). This medical condition causes anything from bloating and nausea to loss of fertility, organ failure, and death. And as *Time* magazine recently highlighted, the long-term risks to egg donors are unknown for the simple reason that "they have never actually been studied." Wonder of wonders.

In one of the few studies actually on record, Dr. Jennifer Schneider and Wendy Kramer surveyed 155 egg donors about some of the long-term outcomes from their donation experience. They found that almost one-third of donors suffered health complications associated with OHSS, and 5 percent suffered subsequent infertility.

It goes without saying that because the long-term risks of egg donation are essentially unknown, the donors' "informed consent" at the time of donation is a joke.

Nonetheless, when looking at the prospect of $5,000 to $10,000, most low-income women are not going to care. That's why paying women for eggs will necessarily lead to the undue inducement and consequent exploitation of women. A voluntary donor, by contrast, is much more likely to calmly weigh the pros and cons of donation, and only go through with it if she feels strongly that she is doing good.

It's not surprising that egg-donation agencies across the country are reporting a sharp increase in applicants seeking to donate eggs, as high as 55 percent in some places compared with the same period last year. Is that due to a sharp increase in altruism? I don't think so. "Whenever the employment rate is down, we get more calls." That's what Robin von Halle, president of Alternative Reproductive Resources, a Chicago-based fertility clinic, told the *Wall Street Journal* last December. "We're even getting men offering up their wives; it's pretty scary," she said.

And by the way: What would those donated eggs be used for? Everything from creating human embryos specifically for research purposes to attempts at human cloning. New York could pave the way for all these practices by making egg donations fundable with state tax dollars. Maybe your state will follow suit.

Periodical Bibliography

The following articles have been selected to supplement the diverse views presented in this chapter.

Ronald Bailey — "Fresh (Human) Eggs for Sale," *Reason*, October 11, 2011.

Anette Breindl — "Human Egg Cells Reprogrammed, but for Now, with Extra Genome," *BioWorld Today*, October 6, 2011.

W. Malcolm Byrnes — "A Biomedical Revolution: The Pro-Life Promise of a New Stem Cell Technology," *America*, August 16, 2010.

Stephen Cauchi — "Clone Rangers: Cell Scientists Tackle Balding One Hair at a Time," *Sydney Morning Herald*, May 1, 2011.

M.D.R. Evans and Jonathan Kelley — "US Attitudes Toward Human Embryonic Stem Cell Research," *Nature Biotechnology*, June 2011.

Uta Grieshammer, Kelly A. Shepard, Elizabeth A. Nigh, and Alan Trounson — "Finding the Niche for Human Somatic Cell Nuclear Transfer," *Nature Biotechnology*, August 2011.

Arlene Judith Klotzko — "Regenerating a Stem-Cell Ethics Debate," *New Scientist*, October 17, 2011.

William B. Neaves — "When Does a Person Become a Person?," *National Catholic Reporter*, December 26, 2008.

Rob Stein — "Scientists Report Possibly Crucial Advance in Human Embryonic Stem Cell Research," *Washington Post*, October 5, 2011.

Nicholas Wade — "After Setbacks in Harvesting Stem Cells, a New Approach Shows Promise," *New York Times*, October 5, 2011.

CHAPTER 2

What Ethical and Moral Issues Surround Reproductive Cloning?

Chapter Preface

Randolfe Wicker has been a gay rights activist since the 1950s. A member of one of the first gay rights organizations in the United States, the Mattachine Society, Wicker has spoken out for gay rights at every turn. The Internet contains a number of references to Randolfe Wicker, such as a 1997 interview with the *New York Times*, an article on the website Gaytoday.com, and the home page of the pro-cloning group Clone Rights United Front. Wicker created the organization to promote human cloning, particularly as a reproductive option for gay and lesbian couples. The organization's website, Clone rights.com, has not been updated in several years. However, the notion that same-sex couples can benefit from human reproductive cloning still remains.

Generally, the options available to same-sex couples who desire children are the same as for infertile heterosexual couples. They can try to adopt a child or use an assisted reproductive technology to try to conceive a genetically related child. Assisted reproductive technologies give people in same-sex relationships choices in creating their own genetically related family. Lesbian couples can find a sperm donor and use in vitro fertilization to have a child genetically related to one of them. For men in same-sex relationships, surrogacy is an option. In this case, egg cells from a donor are fertilized with sperm from one of the men; the resulting embryos are implanted into the uterus of a surrogate. On the website of the Center for Surrogate Parenting Inc., a gay man named Brian shares his feelings about wanting to become a parent and choosing surrogacy to conceive a child:

> In our fifth year together, Craig and I decided to start a family. We considered all our options, and settled on surrogacy as a means of having a child. From the beginning, we were hyper-aware of the challenges facing us as gay parents,

and sensitive to how different our child might feel with two dads. Deep inside, however, we've never doubted we were doing the right thing. What could be more wondrous than creating and nurturing a little life.[1]

Cloning, if used for reproductive purposes, is a type of assisted reproductive technology. The cloning process, called somatic cell nuclear transfer, or SCNT, requires an unfertilized female egg. Just as the name of the procedure implies, the nucleus of the egg cell is removed and replaced with the nucleus of an adult cell, such as a skin cell, from the individual wishing to be cloned. Using chemicals or electricity, scientists "stimulate" the egg cell to begin dividing just as if it were a fertilized egg. The egg would then be implanted into a woman's uterus and allowed to develop into a new baby girl or boy. The child would have the DNA of the individual who provided the skin cell. However, he or she would also carry a tiny amount of DNA from the donor of the unfertilized egg cell.

With reproductive cloning, same-sex couples could be more involved in the creation of the child. Cloning would eliminate the need for lesbian couples to rely on a sperm donor. Additionally, cloning provides opportunities for both women to directly participate in the creation of the child. One woman could provide the egg cell and the other woman could provide the skin cell for cloning. The fertilized egg could be implanted in either woman.

For gay men, reproductive cloning would allow a couple to have a child with the DNA of mostly one of the men and only a tiny amount from the egg donor. However, they would still need to rely on a woman to be a surrogate and carry the baby. Gene splicing, a technology used to combine DNA from two different individuals, may in the future provide gay men the opportunity to have a child sharing both men's DNA. In a January 2011 paper, Erez Aloni, a Center for Reproductive Rights–Columbia Law School fellow at the University of Pennsylvania Law School, discussed the impact reproductive cloning could have on the lesbian, gay, bisexual, transgender, and intersex (LGBTI) community. According to Aloni, "cloning technologies may be uniquely positioned to offer a new kind of reproductive 'future' for LGBTI people—one that is neither identical to nor wholly apart from the culture of the past. . . . It has far-reaching implications that fundamentally challenge the binary system of sexuality."[2] On the Clonerights.com website, Randolfe Wicker contends that "cloning renders heterosexuality's historic monopoly on reproduction obsolete."[3]

There are many people who oppose reproductive cloning based on ethical and moral concerns. Some people believe it is wrong to meddle with human life at its earliest stages, while others believe human cloning goes against nature. Still others worry about the fate of cloned humans. There are also those who specifically oppose reproductive cloning by gays or lesbians.

The possibility that reproductive cloning can enable same-sex couples to have genetically related children is only one of several contentious debates surrounding reproductive cloning. In the following chapter of Opposing Viewpoints: Cloning, the contributors discuss other ethical and moral concerns about reproductive cloning.

Notes

1. "A Special Story—Brian and Craig," Center for Surrogate Parenting Inc., www.creatingfamilies.com.
2. Erez Aloni, "Cloning and the LGBTI Family: Cautious Optimism," New York University Review of Law & Social Change, May 22, 2011.
3. Randolfe Wicker, "To Heterodoxy Magazine: Randolfe Wicker, Evaluates Christopher Rapp's Article and Re-Phrases Himself, Saying: 'Cloning Renders Heterosexuality's Monopoly on Reproduction Obsolete,'" Clone Rights United Front, www.clonerights.com/hetrodoxy.htm.

> *"Nature wants us to pass on our genes; if cloning assists in that effort, nature would not be offended."*

Embrace Human Cloning

Gregg Easterbrook

In the following viewpoint, Gregg Easterbrook argues that reproductive cloning is ethical. Easterbrook argues that cloning is not offensive to nature. Instead, he says, nature produces clones all the time, and the passing on of genes, which cloning does, is "natural." Easterbrook says there are some issues to consider about reproductive cloning; however, it should not be dismissed as being unnatural or unethical. Gregg Easterbrook is an American writer, lecturer, and a senior editor of the New Republic. *His books include* A Moment on the Earth: The Coming Age of Environmental Optimism *and* The Progress Paradox: How Life Gets Better While People Feel Worse.

As you read, consider the following questions:

1. What is Easterbrook referring to when he says chances are you already know a clone?

2. According to Easterbrook, what reason does Leon Kass give for arguing that human cloning is offensive?

3. What reproductive technology does Easterbrook say was once seen as depraved God-playing?

Why shouldn't science create carbon copies of people? Nature does it every day.

Human clones, it is widely assumed, would be monstrous perversions of nature. Yet chances are you already know one. Indeed, you may know several and even have dated a clone. They walk among us in the form of identical twins: people who share exact sets of DNA. Such twins almost always look alike and often have similar quirks. But their minds, experiences, and personalities are different, and no one supposes they are less than fully human. And if identical twins are fully human, wouldn't cloned people be as well?

Suppose scientists could create a clone from an adult human: It would probably be more distinct from its predecessor than most identical twins are from each other. A clone from a grown-up would have the same DNA but would come into the world as a gurgling baby, not an instant adult, as in sci-fi. The clone would go through childhood and adolescence with the same life-shaping unpredictability as any kid.

The eminent University of Chicago ethicist Leon Kass has argued that human cloning would be offensive in part because the clone would "not be fully a surprise to the world." True, but what child is? Almost all share physical traits and mannerisms with their parents. By having different experiences than their parents (er, parent) and developing their own personalities, clones would become distinct individuals with the same originality and dignity as identical twins—or anyone else.

Others argue that cloning is "unnatural." But nature wants us to pass on our genes; if cloning assists in that effort, nature would not be offended. Moreover, cloning itself isn't new; there have been many species that reproduced clonally and a few that still do. And there's nothing intrinsically unnatural

Fear of the Unnatural

These fears make little sense in themselves; some invoke more or less magical thinking. But their pull is relentless. Why do we insist that this "otherness" and this intervention in procreation are only steps towards a Brave New World? Partly, I think, it is a defence against the uncomfortable notion that we can be "manufactured". But at root, making people (or merely appearing to do so, as in IVF [in vitro fertilisation] and reproductive cloning) is arguably the ultimate "unnatural" act.

Philip Ball, "It's Alive, I Tell You!,"
New Scientist, *February 12, 2011.*

about human inventions that improve reproductive odds—does anyone think nature is offended by hospital delivery made safe by banks of machines?

Nature Wants Us to Pass On Our Genes. Cloning Assists in That Effort.

This does not necessarily make human cloning desirable; there are complicated issues to consider. Initial mammalian cloning experiments, with sheep and other species, have produced many sickly offspring that die quickly. Could it ever be ethical to conduct research that produces sick babies in the hope of figuring out how to make healthy clones? And clones might be treated as inferiors, rendering them unhappy.

Still, human cloning should not be out of the question. In vitro fertilization was once seen as depraved God-playing and is now embraced, even by many of the devoutly religious. Cloning could be a blessing for the infertile, who otherwise could not experience biological parenthood. And, of course, it would be a blessing for the clone itself. Suppose a clone is later asked, "Are you glad you exist even though you are physically quite similar to someone else, or do you wish you had never existed?" We all know what the answer would be.

| "Cloning is an affront to the dignity of
  human beings."

Human Reproductive Cloning Is Ethically Problematic

Dennis P. Hollinger

In the following viewpoint, an excerpt from his book The Meaning of Sex: Christian Ethics and the Moral Life, *Dennis P. Hollinger argues that human reproductive cloning is ethically wrong. Hollinger says the cloning of a human being completely separates sex, love, and procreation, reducing the value of the family. Additionally, maintains Hollinger, cloning is ethically problematic because it turns procreation into manufacturing. According to Hollinger, reproductive cloning is an affront to human dignity. Dennis P. Hollinger is president and the Colman M. Mockler Distinguished Professor of Christian Ethics at Gordon-Conwell Theological Seminary.*

As you read, consider the following questions:

1. What is the fifth reason that Hollinger gives for why some people might desire reproductive cloning?

Dennis P. Hollinger, *The Meaning of Sex: Christian Ethics and the Moral Life*, Baker Publishing Group, 2009, pp. 218–222. Copyright © 2009 by Baker Academic, a division of Baker Publishing Group. All rights reserved. Reproduced by permission.

2. What reason does Hollinger give for asserting that society should have an interest in keeping sex, love, and procreation together?

3. According to Hollinger, who said "parents never get the children they thought they were giving birth to"?

With cloning we come to the ultimate of reproductive control. In this technology we not only bypass sex, but, unlike other ARTs [assisted reproductive technologies], we bypass the sexual gametes, egg and sperm. In fact males are no longer needed at all. All that is required is a female egg and a transplanted cell from a donor of either sex. This is truly asexual reproduction, and with the birth of Dolly the sheep in 1996 (the first cloned mammal), reproductive cloning is no longer just the subject of science fiction. It is a reality whose time has come.

With cloning we enter a brave new world of reproduction that is radically different from all previous forms. We enter an unknown world in its effects, and a revolutionary world in terms of its ethical and social implications. As the President's Council on Bioethics put it, cloning is something "that touches fundamental aspects of our humanity. The notion of cloning raises issues about identity and individuality, the meaning of having children, the difference between procreation and manufacture, and the relationship between the generations." . . .

The Technology and Purposes of Cloning

Cloning of both animals and humans looks fairly simple on paper, but making it happen is not so easy.

It is accomplished by removing the nucleus of a female egg and replacing it with nuclear material from any cell (other than gamete cells) of a donor. The process is technically called somatic cell nuclear transfer (SCNT) and stands in contrast to the conventional conception of bringing two gamete cells (egg and sperm) together. When the nucleus of the donor is placed into the ovum, an electrical charge is administered with the intent that the ovum, with the new nuclear material, will begin to divide, as if impregnated by a male sperm. From there on the biological development is essentially the same as normal modes of conception, embryonic/fetal development, and birth. The clone (animal or human) is virtually a genetic duplicate of the donor of the nucleus. In human cloning, the clone would clearly be a human person, but a genetic twin of the person providing the nucleus.

There are essentially two forms of cloning in terms of intent: therapeutic cloning and reproductive cloning. Or as some prefer: cloning for biomedical research and cloning to produce children. In therapeutic cloning the purpose is to develop a clone from which researchers can garner stem cells for research and therapy, or gain scientific knowledge for curing human diseases. In reproductive cloning the intention is to initiate a pregnancy with the hope of producing a child. At this time most of the stated interest is for biomedical research and therapy. Therapeutic cloning can produce stem cells that have the potential of healing various diseases. The interest in cloning for stem cells centers on overcoming immune rejection, which is a major barrier to stem cell transplant. With therapeutic cloning the donor nucleus could come from the patient needing the stem cell transplant, thus overcoming the immune rejection. In the process the cloned human embryo is destroyed.

Our major focus here, however, is on reproductive cloning. . . . Why would one desire reproductive cloning? There are several reasons. One purpose might be to provide an infertile couple the possibility of having a child that is biologically related to one of the individuals in the dyad. A second reason might be to "replicate" or "bring back" a loved one who died. If the nuclear material was taken from the deceased person, the clone would be genetically identical to the dead person. A third rationale might be to have a child without a genetic disease. If both persons had a recessive gene for a genetic disease, cloning could ensure that the offspring would not have the disorder. A fourth reason for human cloning would be to provide a transplant organ or tissue for a sick or dying person. With a clone of the sick person there would be a genetic match that could provide the transplant material without risk of rejection. A fifth reason for cloning is eugenic purposes. Here the intent would be to reproduce an extremely gifted, talented, or intelligent human being. A final rationale could be scientific knowledge. Scientists have long debated the nature versus nurture issue, and cloning would provide interesting insight in that the clone and donor would not be living in identical contexts or have the same experiences. It could also provide useful knowledge about the transmission and course of various diseases.

It is one thing to have reasons for cloning. But the ethics of it all is another matter.

At present most researchers and bioethicists believe that reproductive cloning would be ethically wrong. But many add, "At this point." The crucial moral issue for many is the harm that would come to the clone and to the cloned embryos in the research process. As [ethicist] Roger Shinn puts it, "The statistics of risk are foreboding. In the case of Dolly, [Ian] Wilmut needed 277 attempts. Only 29 resulted in embryos that survived more than six days. These led to thirteen pregnancies. All miscarried, some with malformations, except Dolly." In the end Dolly developed serious physiological problems and had to be euthanized. It is generally believed that with humans the results would be even more formidable.

But not all accept this risk assumption. Some researchers seem determined to be the first to clone a live human being—a drive that has led to fraudulent claims and laying aside ethical concerns. One aspiring cloner, Dr. Panayiotis Zavos, told *Time* magazine, "Ethics is a wonderful word, but we need look beyond the ethical issues here. [Cloning is] not an ethical issue. It's a medical issue. We have a duty here. Some people need this to complete the life cycle, to reproduce." Given the keen interest in reproductive cloning by such researchers, and the drive toward therapeutic cloning (which is a step in the direction of reproductive cloning), it seems only a matter of time till someone will lay aside the concerns for harm and produce a human clone. But even if we could control for harm and risk, should we do it?

Significant Concerns

From a sexual ethics standpoint there are significant concerns with reproductive cloning. In the cloning of a human being by asexual means, we have the most radical separation of sex, love, and procreation. As I have contended throughout this [viewpoint], God designed that humans come into the world out of the most loving, one-flesh intimacy possible—sexual intercourse of a husband and wife. To be sure, our society has frequently pulled apart this unity with the large numbers of children born outside of wedlock. Artificial insemination and surrogacy sever the unity of sex, love, and procreation as well. But with cloning the three are pulled apart to the fullest degree. With other ART there is still the "stuff" (egg and sperm) of sex in procreation, but with cloning we render even the "stuff" of sex obsolete. This is not merely a theological argument regarding God's designs for humanity. Society itself ought to have an interest in keeping sex, love, and procreation together for the good of the social order.

The separation of this triad in cloning potentially turns procreation into an individualistic enterprise, resulting from individual choices. The family, the moral context for procreation, is virtually absent in the pursuit of this form of procreative liberty. Brent Waters notes, "The problem with procreative liberty is its presumption that a child is an outcome of reproductive choices." In contrast, he proposes that "we think of children as the culmination of a complex and purposeful

Most Americans Think Cloning Humans Is Morally Wrong

	Morally acceptable %	Morally wrong %
Doctor-assisted suicide	45	48
Abortion	39	51
Having a baby outside of marriage	54	41
Buying and wearing clothing made of animal fur	56	39
Gay or lesbian relations	56	39
Medical testing on animals	55	38
Sex between an unmarried man and a woman	60	36
Cloning animals	32	62
Medical research using stem cells obtained from human embryos	62	30
Gambling	64	31
Pornography	30	66
The death penalty	65	28
Divorce	69	23
Suicide	15	80
Cloning humans	12	84
Polygamy, when a married person has more than one spouse at the same time	11	86
Married men and women having an affair	7	91

TAKEN FROM: Lydia Saad, "Doctor-Assisted Suicide Is Moral Issue Dividing Americans Most," Gallup, Inc., May 31, 2011. www.gallup.com.

process, and that procreation itself be viewed as a teleologically ordered pattern of practices. Children, then, are more the outgrowth of a relationship than the outcome of individual decisions." In individually determining ahead of time the exact result of procreation, cloning is "incompatible with the family as a place of unconditional belonging," says Waters. Moreover, "The family is built upon the one-flesh unity of a wife and husband, who out of the totality of their shared being bring into life a new being who is part of them and yet who is also wholly other than them."

All of this leads to another way in which cloning is ethically problematic. It is the most explicit form of turning procreation into manufacturing. We have already noted that the language of reproduction connotes manufacturing, which intentionally creates a desired, predetermined outcome. Cloning is the ultimate of reproductive manufacturing in that one determines ahead of time the exact result of the procreative process. The President's Council on Bioethics sharply contrasts the traditional and natural mode of procreation with the cloning and manufacturing mode. In the traditional and natural form,

> The precise genetic endowment of each child is determined by a combination of nature and chance, not by human design: each human child naturally acquires and shares the common human species genotype, each child is genetically (equally) kin to each (both) parent(s), yet each child is also genetically unique. Cloning to produce children departs from this pattern. A cloned child has unilineal, not bilineal, descent; he or she is genetically kin to only one progenitor. . . .

In God's designs for procreation, children are not a product. Children are a gift flowing from the one-flesh, loving relationship—the most secure context for entering this world and being nurtured to fullness of life.

Thus, cloning is an affront to the dignity of human beings, which flows from creation in God's image. It undermines the unique individuality (not individualism) which is part of the *imago Dei* and human worth. It is not mere twinning as some advocates claim, for it is an intentional twinning in which twin sister is also mother. It compounds family and generational relations, potentially causing significant identity and relational issues.

Cloning also contradicts the very nature of parenting from a biblical perspective. [Theologian] Will Willimon sums it up well:

> Parents never get the children they thought they were giving birth to. That's why I'm unhappy with the term "planned parenthood," as if it's only desirable to have children if you have planned or chosen them. Who plans to have a severely retarded child, or a rebellious child, or a child who plays the drums in a rock band? Sometimes we get such a child. And what then? You can choose an automobile, but you can't choose a child. You must receive a child. The Bible says a child is a gift, not a possession or a project.

Parenting is not about our own self-willed determinations, which is the very nature of cloning. It is a stewardship flowing from the one-flesh, procreative, loving relationship of marriage. In procreation and parenting we are hospitable to the children God gives, not the children we have designed for our own selfish ends.

> "The freedom of infertile couples to use cloning is weightier than the arguments against it."

Reproductive Cloning by Infertile Couples Is Ethical

Carson Strong

In the following viewpoint, ethicist Carson Strong explains and defends his view that reproductive cloning, if it is able to be performed safely, is an ethical option for infertile couples. Strong believes that cloning provides a way for infertile couples to participate in the creation of a person, and the genetic and biological connection provided by cloning may have special significance to some couples. He believes these reasons for cloning carry more importance than any argument against it. Strong addresses specific objections to his opinion put forth by two other ethicists, and he concludes that their arguments are not logical or persuasive. Carson Strong is a professor in the Department of Human Values and Ethics at the University of Tennessee's College of Medicine. He is the author of Ethics in Reproductive and Perinatal Medicine: A New Framework.

As you read, consider the following questions:

1. In discussing whether it would be ethically permissible for infertile couples to use cloning, how does Strong pose the issue?

2. Aside from reproductive cloning, what other assisted reproductive technologies does Strong believe many infertile couples would pursue instead of adoption?

3. According to Strong, permitting cloning because it provides infertile couples a way to have genetically related children supports the notion that genetic makeup, and not what, determines an individual's characteristics?

In several writings, I have defended reproductive cloning as an option for infertile couples, with qualifications. At present there is a compelling reason to prohibit attempts at human reproductive cloning; namely, there is evidence that there is a high probability that the child would have congenital anomalies so severe as to make the procreation wrongful. But in the future, advances in the technology of cloning might make it possible to create children with no increased risk of anomalies compared to procreation by sexual intercourse. I have argued that, if reproductive cloning could be performed with such a relatively low risk of anomalies, it would be ethically permissible for infertile couples to use it as a way to have genetically related children and that such use should not be prohibited.

Neil Levy and Mianna Lotz have raised objections to my defence of such cloning, and they have offered new arguments against it. In doing so, they have made a useful contribution to the ongoing international debate over the ethics of human reproductive cloning. One main thrust of their criticism is to reject the idea, for which I argued, that the desire to have genetically related children can be defensible. They hold that the view that it can be reasonable to desire genetic children is not only 'erroneous' but also 'pernicious' because it leads to undesirable consequences. One of the bad consequences, they claim, is that the availability of cloning will diminish the number of adoptions and thereby adversely affect the interests of children who need to be adopted. To examine their criticisms, it will be helpful to begin with their arguments against the view that it can be reasonable to desire genetically related children. To provide a context for this discussion, let me briefly summarize the arguments I had given.

Reasons to Desire Genetic Offspring

In discussing whether it would be ethically permissible for infertile couples to use cloning, assuming it could be performed without an elevated risk of anomalies, I posed the issue as follows: 'Which is weightier, infertile couples' reproductive freedom to use cloning or the arguments against cloning humans?' In addressing this question, I drew upon earlier work in which I had examined the more general question of why we should consider procreative freedom to be valuable. I had asked, 'Is it solely because freedom in general is valuable, or is there special significance to the fact that the freedom in question is *reproductive*?' To explore this question, I focused on the type of procreation commonly referred to as 'having a child of one's own', sometimes stated simply as 'having a child' or 'having children'. Specifically, I used these expressions to refer to begetting a child by sexual intercourse whom one rears or helps rear. This is the common form of procreation in which parents raise children who are genetically their own.

Although a desire for genetic children is widespread, some have held that no good reason can be given in support of such desire. Rather than simply accept that view, I suggested that we should consider whether there are defensible reasons that could be given by persons for having such a desire. Because having children by means of the common form of procreation involves having genetically related children, I suggested that some insight could be gained by asking whether good reasons can be given for valuing procreation in the common situation. I identified six reasons that persons could give in support of a desire to procreate in the common scenario. This was not intended as an exhaustive list of reasons, but to show that reasons can be given that merit consideration and that are neither trivial, vain, nor confused. These are reasons that, for some people at least, can contribute to the personal meaningfulness of having children. These reasons are as follows: having a genetic child in the common scenario involves participation in the creation of a person; it can be an affirmation of a couple's mutual love and acceptance of each other; it can contribute to sexual intimacy; it provides a type of link to future persons; it involves experiences of pregnancy and childbirth; and it leads to experiences associated with child rearing. I held that some couples might attach some of these meanings to their procreation, and that these meanings can promote the well-being of some couples by contributing to self-identity and self-fulfillment. . . . The fact that there are such reasons supports the view that freedom to pursue ordinary procreation is valuable not simply because freedom in general is valuable, but also because ordinary procreation has features that can give it a special significance to procreators.

In exploring whether the freedom of infertile couples to use cloning as a way to have a child genetically related to one of them should be valued, I summarized and cited my previous discussion of the value of procreative freedom. I then considered the extent to which the six identified reasons could be applicable to the cloning context. Among the reasons that deal specifically with there being a genetic or biological connection, I focused on two: cloning would permit the couple to participate in the creation of a person, and for some infertile couples doing so might have personal meaning; and for some couples, the genetic and biological connection provided by cloning might be regarded as giving their procreation a special

Reproductive Cloning Can Benefit the LGBTI Community

Prospective parents in the LGBTI [lesbian, gay, bisexual, transgender, and intersex] community face a number of obstacles. Cloning—to the extent that it is safe and available—could present a better alternative than the options currently available to those who prefer a genetically related child. It could provide an easier way to have such a child with minimal involvement of third parties. Combined with gene splicing, it might allow for LGBTI couples, or even close friends, to have a child who carries the mixed genes of both parties. In order for such possibilities to become a reality, however, we need further research. Members of the LGBTI community should express their interest in this research to ensure that they are not ultimately excluded from the opportunity to use it.

Erez Aloni,
"Cloning and the LGBTI Family: Cautious Optimism,"
New York University Review of Law & Social Change,
May 22, 2011.

significance as an affirmation of mutual love and acceptance. Admittedly, there are methods other than cloning, such as gamete or embryo donation, in which infertile couples can participate in the creation of a person or affirm their mutual love. Cloning is *a way* to do these things, and the fact that it is a way might contribute to some infertile couples regarding cloning as a desirable form of procreation.

Thus, the freedom of infertile couples to use cloning is valuable because freedom in general is valuable and because reproductive cloning has features, similar to those of the common form of procreation, that—for some couples at least—

can give it meanings that enrich their lives and promote their well-being. In considering the main objections to human reproductive cloning, I argued that in the context of infertility none of them withstands critical examination. I concluded that the freedom of infertile couples to use cloning is weightier than the arguments against it.

Participating in the Creation of a Person

Levy and Lotz object to my argument that cloning could have a special meaning for some infertile couples because it involves participation in the creation of a person. They begin their argument by claiming that it is unclear what I meant by 'participation in the creation of a person'. They opine that I might have simply meant 'conception' or that I might have been referring to the influence of social parents on a child's development. In reply, the term 'conception' does not seem to be apt, for it is commonly used to refer to the union of sperm and ovum, which does not take place in cloning. Moreover, the question of what I meant by 'participation in the creation of a person', in the context in question, was addressed in my article. I stated:

> The person whose chromosomes are used would participate by providing the genetic material for the new person. Regardless of whose chromosomes are used, if the woman is capable of gestating, she could participate by gestating and giving birth to the child.

Apparently overlooking this statement, Levy and Lotz argue as follows:

> If by 'creation' Strong simply has in mind 'conception', then there is no sense in which people who decide to have a biological child are—by dint of bringing about conception—engaged in the creation of a 'person'.

Their statement is incorrect, for there certainly is a sense in which conception, assuming there is normal development, plays a role in the creation of a person. Conception—that is, the union of sperm and ovum following sexual intercourse or during in vitro fertilization—brings into being an individual that, in the normal course of events, will develop into a person. Without the initial coming into being, the person in question would not exist.

In cloning, the bringing into being takes place through somatic cell nuclear transfer. If a couple has a child through cloning, their decision to do so and their taking the necessary steps is certainly a participation in the creation of a person. To provide the chromosomes and to gestate are specific ways of participating. So, it is a mistake to think that those who create a child through cloning are not participating in the creation of a person. . . .

Levy and Lotz also object to my argument that cloning could have a special meaning for some couples who might view creating a child in this way as an affirmation of their mutual love and acceptance. The attempted rebuttal, however, goes off course at the very beginning because Levy and Lotz state my argument incorrectly. Specifically, they characterize my argument as stating that 'biological parenting *is* the expression and affirmation of a couple's love for one another'. That statement, which uses 'is' instead of a more appropriate phrase such as 'can be', is mistaken because it implies that in *all* cases having children has that significance for procreators. . . .

Thus, although Levy and Lotz have perhaps defeated some arguments that I never presented, they have not provided any valid arguments that would even count against, much less defeat, the arguments I actually gave. Therefore, their claim to have shown that there are no valid arguments supporting the use of reproductive cloning by infertile couples is entirely unsupported.

Cloning's Impact on Adoption

In addition to arguing that the reasons supporting reproductive cloning are unsound, Levy and Lotz offer several arguments for the view that such cloning is 'pernicious' because it would be harmful on balance and should not be permitted. Of particular interest is their argument based on the impact of reproductive cloning on adoption. Virtually every infertile couple who turns to assisted reproduction has considered the possibility of adoption, and Levy and Lotz should be commended for making this option explicit in the debate. They assert that '[i]f cloning were to become widely available, the primary motive for adoption would be removed'. They then state that, because there would be fewer adoptions, the result would be 'an overall diminution in the satisfaction of needs (or desires or preferences)'. In response, several points can be made. First, there is a problem that often arises with arguments that appeal to the long-term overall social consequences of a proposed public policy. Namely, it is difficult to predict accurately what the long-term consequences are going to be, and this problem is exacerbated when the policy pertains to a technology that probably will not be available, if ever, until quite some time into the future, as is the case presumably with reproductive cloning. Of course, the plight of children who could benefit from being adopted is of great concern. But would forbidding cloning really play an important role in helping such children? The answer would depend on a number of variables that are difficult to predict: the extent to which infertile couples would want to use cloning; the extent to which, if cloning were prohibited, infertile couples would turn to other forms of assisted reproductive technology (ART) instead of adoption; the extent to which social problems that contribute to children being given up for adoption are addressed; the extent to which there are public campaigns to encourage adoption; and the extent to which rules for adoption are made less or more restrictive, among other variables. Given such uncertainties, is there really a basis for claiming, as Levy and Lotz seem to do, that cloning would have a significant impact on adoption? Isn't it at least as plausible to think that, if cloning is forbidden, many infertile couples would choose gamete or embryo donation rather than adoption?

Another problem is that their argument seems to involve a misplaced focus if one wants to come up with ways to help children who need to be adopted. There are more direct ways to do this, such as bringing the needs of specific children to the public's attention, offering more public resources to help adoptive parents rear difficult-to-place children such as children with handicaps, perhaps offering reduced-cost health care for adopted children, reducing barriers to lesbian and gay couples who want to adopt, and so on. Such measures could have an impact that might be felt long before we ever reach the point of being able to clone people without an elevated risk of anomalies.

Yet another problem with Levy and Lotz's argument is that it also applies to the various forms of ART. If cloning should be prohibited in an attempt to help children who would benefit from adoption, then to be consistent should not one also advocate the banning of donor insemination, ovum donation, controlled ovarian stimulation, and in vitro fertilization? All of these provide alternatives to adoption. If banning cloning would increase adoptions, would not banning these forms of ART also increase adoptions? Thus, Levy and Lotz's argument seems to have consequences for procreative freedom that are more pronounced than one might initially think. . . .

Additional Arguments

Levy and Lotz also argue that permitting cloning will reinforce a mistaken 'proprietarian' attitude—that is, the view that genetic parents own their children. They state, 'we might plausibly think that permitting cloning in a context in which the genetic is over-valued will give proprietarian attitudes more "leash" than is desirable'. In reply, stating their argument more fully will show its weakness. Levy and Lotz seem to be claiming that people will draw an inference that goes something like this: 'Permitting cloning in part because it provides infertile couples a way to have genetically related children supports the idea that genetic parents own their children'. The problem is that the inference in question is erroneous. It is one thing to desire genetic children, and it is something else entirely to believe that one owns one's genetic offspring. Thus, it is a mistake to think that a policy of permitting cloning in part because it is a way to have genetically related children implies that genetic parents own their children. . . .

Another argument by Levy and Lotz is that permitting cloning will reinforce the mistaken view that genes determine who we are and how we end up in life, and that this mistaken view 'will be used to buttress opposition to, or at least a reduction in, the use of public funds to improve the life prospects of the disadvantaged'. By 'disadvantaged', Levy and Lotz seem to have in mind primarily the poor, but perhaps others as well. In reply, several familiar problems arise. Levy and Lotz seem to be claiming that people will make an inference that goes something like this: 'Permitting cloning in part because it provides infertile couples a way to have genetically related children supports the idea that genetic makeup, and not environment, determines our characteristics.' Again, the inference in question is mistaken. To desire genetic children is entirely different from believing that genes determine who we are. So, it is erroneous to think that a policy of permitting cloning in part because it is an option for having genetically related children implies that genetics determines our characteristics. . . .

In conclusion, Levy and Lotz have failed to show that there are problems with the arguments I put forward in support of the view that, with certain qualifications, use of reproductive cloning by infertile couples would be ethically permissible and should be permitted. They join others who hold that a genetic connection can have no importance without giving good reasons for that view. Moreover, there are serious problems with each of the direct arguments they give against human reproductive cloning. So, they also join a large chorus who oppose all human reproductive cloning without giving good reasons.

"There are two distinct claims on liberty in the case of human reproductive cloning: the parents' right to reproductive freedom and the clones' right to self-determination."

The Rights of Cloned Children Must Be Considered in Reproductive Cloning

Joyce C. Havstad

In the following viewpoint, Joyce C. Havstad asserts that the rights of cloned children must be considered when examining the ethics of reproductive cloning. Havstad acknowledges that the right to procreative autonomy means that individuals have a right to reproduce by means of cloning. However, cloned children also have a right to self-determination, says Havstad, and neither right should outweigh the other. According to Havstad, this tension between the parents' rights and the cloned children's rights should be considered, and cloned children's rights must be protected. Joyce C. Havstad is a graduate student in philosophy at the University of California, San Diego.

Joyce C. Havstad, "Human Reproductive Cloning: A Conflict of Liberties," *Bioethics*, vol. 24, no. 2, February, 2010, pp. 71–77.

As you read, consider the following questions:

1. According to Havstad, what was the name of the essay wherein Joel Feinberg describes the right to self-determination?

2. Havstad says that Brock, Harris, and others examine the possibility of harm done to a clone by violating its right to self-determination and then they dismiss the concern by utilizing a very particular argument. What is this argument?

3. According to Havstad, what is the name of the principle described by Derek Parfit that says individuals usually appeal to the interests of those whom their acts affect?

Discussion of the ethics of human reproductive cloning is restricted to cases in which whole, individual, sentient humans are made from genetic cloning rather than recombination, and created by artifice rather than nature. Although there are some significant scientific obstacles likely to continue hampering the development of human cloning, assuming that these problems are eventually solved, there are various reasons why individuals might want to produce offspring through cloning technology rather than the more conventional methods. For example, if a husband were to die before a couple had any children, the wife might wish to clone the deceased in order to have a child with her husband's genes. Of course, if the deceased member of the couple was the wife instead, producing the clone would require an egg as well as a surrogate carrier. Cloning might also be a desirable option for infertile couples or for same-sex couples if either party does not wish to have offspring to whom an independent third party has contributed any nuclear DNA. In general, the right to such options would be part of what is commonly referred to as the individual's right to reproductive freedom.

Right to Reproductive Freedom

Several philosophers argue for the acceptability, in principle, of human reproductive cloning on the basis of the right to reproductive freedom. Dan [W.] Brock defines this right:

> A right to reproductive freedom is properly understood to include the right to use various assisted reproductive technologies (ARTs), such as in vitro fertilization (IVF), oocyte donation, and so forth.

This right is part of the right to procreative autonomy, which Ronald Dworkin derives from the American political tradition of personal freedom. There is a history of judicial decisions that presuppose a principle of procreative autonomy, presumably because of a commitment to personal liberty and human dignity, as well as the belief that procreative decisions are fundamental to both. Integrity requires that this principle, applied to cases regarding issues such as abortion and contraception, be applied to other kinds of procreative decisions as well. The constitutional basis for this generalized principle creates the right to procreative autonomy.

Despite its American heritage, and because of its derivation from a commitment to personal liberty and human dignity, Dworkin argues that 'the principle of procreative autonomy, in a broad sense, is embedded in any genuinely democratic culture.' It is a negative right that incurs a duty of non-interference, so any imposition on an individual's procreative decision making constitutes an infringement of their right. As a result, barring any other morally relevant impediments, individuals have a right to pursue their own procreative choices, although it is not the case that anyone is obligated to provide them with the object of their choices.

Accepting that individuals have a right to procreative liberty, along with classifying the decision to employ ARTs as a procreative decision, generates the right to reproductive freedom. Accepting that individuals have a right to reproductive freedom, and classifying human reproductive cloning as an ART, makes reproducing by means of cloning an option that individuals have a right to pursue. Although human reproductive cloning may initially seem like a ridiculous thing to pursue, John Harris points out that it is important to many individuals to have offspring that are related to them and only them. There are several kinds of cases where individuals may be unable to accomplish this except by means of human reproductive cloning. As a result, Harris states that

> ... freedom to clone one's own genes might also be defended as a dimension of procreative autonomy because so many people and agencies have been attracted by the idea of the special nature of genes and have linked the procreative imperative to the genetic imperative.

Perhaps it becomes easier to accept the 'cloning imperative' when it is understood as an expression of the 'genetic imperative'.

But regardless of the motivation behind the desire to pursue human reproductive cloning, Brock, Harris and others argue that in the absence of other relevant moral impediments, individuals ought to be permitted to reproduce by means of cloning. The argument goes something like this: Given the right to procreative autonomy and therefore the right to reproductive freedom, and recognizing that human reproductive cloning counts as a kind of ART protected by these rights, then as long as this kind of cloning is not prohibited by some other appropriate moral code, it is a violation of rights to prevent individuals from choosing to reproduce by means of cloning. The question then arises as to whether choosing to employ human reproductive cloning violates any other viable ethical principles. In particular, I will examine the potential for psychological harms resulting from violations of the right to self-determination.

The Right to Self-Determination

The right to self-determination is the right that all persons have to determine, at least to some extent, their own self. [Joel] Feinberg describes the right to self-determination in an essay entitled 'The Child's Right to an Open Future'. He writes:

> ... the mature adult that the child will become, like all free citizens, has a *right of self-determination*, and that right is violated in advance if certain crucial and irrevocable decisions determining the course of his life are made by anyone else before he has the *capacity of self-determination* himself.

This right is, like both the right to procreative autonomy and the right to reproductive freedom, a negative right. Individuals are not to be prevented from developing into the kind of person that they wish to be. The right to self-determination is also satisfied to a degree, rather than as a simple presence or absence. Obviously, all parents influence their children's development—some more so than others. The idea is that there is an amount of excessive interference which constitutes a violation of the right to self-determination, and that cloning someone and forcing the clone to assume that person's identity is an example of an inappropriately extreme case. This is where the concern with potential psychological harms to cloned children arises.

Although clones should not be unduly hindered by the fact that they share a genome with another person, they may be harmed by the expectation of similarity with the people they have been cloned from. If the parent of a cloned child were to attempt to direct the child's personality, abilities, and interests to mimic whomever it is a genetic replica of, then this would constitute a violation of the cloned child's right to self-determination. And here is where the objection to human reproductive cloning arises. Actually, it applies to all individuals with a shared genome, whether they are naturally produced identical twins or genetically engineered human clones.

Cloning Denies Autonomy and Violates Kant's Ethics

So why must humans be free from the arbitrariness of others, including the imposition of genetic identity? Our self-determination and our autonomy, and consequently the prohibition to restrict this autonomy arbitrarily by any other person, are among the basic ingredients of human existence. It is, in fact, an essential part of the definition of being human. By cloning, the clone creator would deny this autonomy to the clone for purely selfish motives and would therefore violate the ethical maxim, which the great philosopher Immanuel Kant formulated 220 years ago, drawing from his categorical imperative: "Act that you use humanity, whether in your own person or in the person of any other, always at the same time as an end, never merely as a means" (Kant, 1785).

Christof Tannert, "Thou Shalt Not Clone,"
EMBO Reports, *vol. 7, no. 3, 2006.*

The claim is that, based on the right of individuals to self-determination, it is wrong to force a shared identity on any two individuals based on a shared genome. But many authors dismiss this objection.

Dismissing Psychological Harms

There are typically two responses to the threat of the genetic fallacy leading to violations of rights resulting in psychological harms. The first is to point out that the genetic fallacy is, in fact, a fallacy. Authors in favor of human reproductive cloning argue that we need not consider this potential consequence because it would be a mistake for people to assume that a clone will have the same identity as the original person and treat them accordingly. The problem arises from ignorance. Because genetic clones look similar, people tend to assume that they are similar in personality. To commit the fallacy of genetic determinism is [according to Richard Lewontin] to indulge in the 'pervasive error that confuses the genetic state of an organism with its total physical and psychic nature as a human being.' It assumes that genetic identity is equivalent with personal identity, but this is patently false. Identical twins have the same genetic identity and yet are different persons. Clones will have different identities and be different people, just as entitled to their right to ignorance, an open future, and self-determination as naturally created identical twins are.

Unfortunately, people do commit this fallacy and make this assumption. And some might seek to create a genetic clone in order to try and replicate a loved one's personal identity. Someone who desires to recreate another person may be expecting the clone to be similar to the cloned. Someone who is cloning a past person is potentially, by the very act of seeking to clone it, attempting to recreate that identity. But to attempt to replicate people by replicating their genomes is ethically troublesome. It is this tendency, a human predilection for this motivation for cloning, that must be considered when one examines the morality of the practice.

I conclude that the psychological harms that may be done to a clone whose parents commit the fallacy of genetic determinism ought to be considered even though it is a mistake to think that genetic identity and personal identity are the same. This is because although it is a mistake to commit the genetic fallacy, some may still commit that mistake, resulting in psychological harms. These harms are morally relevant despite that they result from a misunderstanding of the relationship between genetics and identity. Simply pointing out that to commit the genetic fallacy is, in fact, to commit a fallacy, is not sufficient to address the threat of psychological harms to clones.

Several authors employ a second strategy in order to override concerns with a cloned individual's rights. Brock, Harris, and others each contemplate the difficulties raised by Feinberg. . . . They each examine the possibility of harm done to a clone by violating its right to self-determination. Then they dismiss the concern by utilizing a very particular argument, [Derek] Parfit's non-identity problem. Parfit's non-identity problem explores the difficulty in talking about actions that determine both the existence and quality of life of future persons. He points out that our choices today often have two types of effects: quality-of-life effects (ones that affect the experiences of potential future persons) and reproductive effects (ones that affect who are the actual future persons). When we talk about choices that have an effect on who is born, there is a problem with discussing an additional effect on their quality of life because they would not exist were we to do otherwise. Parfit states that it is inappropriate to talk about a future person being harmed by a choice that negatively affects his quality of life, but without which he would not exist. Because of this he concludes that in cases with reproductive effects we cannot talk about harm to future persons in person-affecting terms.

The decision to allow or prohibit human reproductive cloning obviously has a reproductive effect. The non-identity problem reveals that it is inappropriate to appeal to potential psychological harms as grounds for prohibiting it. This is because although the decision to clone a child may indeed lead to its right to self-determination being violated, unless this goes so far as to make the clone's life not worth living, the decision did not actually harm the child, since it would not exist otherwise. Brock explains this claim: 'the later twin is not harmed by being given a life even with these psychological burdens, since the alternative of never existing at all is arguably worse'. Raanan Gillon asks, 'What is preferable for that child? To exist but to have those problems, or not to exist at all?'

The Non-Identity Problem

I think there are some very important points to be made about using the non-identity problem to dismiss the possibility of psychological harms. First, I would like to point out that despite his non-identity problem, Parfit still thinks that we can morally object to choices that have both negative quality-of-life and reproductive effects. He explains:

> Many writers claim that, in causing such effects, we would be acting against the interests of future people. Given the point about personal identity, this is not true. But I was inclined to think that this made no moral difference. The objection to these . . . choices seemed to me just as strong.

Parfit's main point is that these objections appeal to an uncertain and unfamiliar principle that we have yet to articulate. He writes that 'we will need some wider claim to cover these. Call this claim (X). I am not sure what (X) should be.' But he very specifically states that 'I would not *want* people to conclude that we can be less concerned about the more remote effects of our social policies.' So Parfit himself would not want his non-identity problem to be used to dismiss concern over the potential psychological harms that cloning could incur on future children.

Second, it ought to be noted that Parfit has merely demonstrated that our usual way of talking about moral responsibilities—in terms of harm to another—fails to represent our concern for the welfare of future persons in these cases. Parfit's non-identity problem does not prove that we have no moral responsibilities in these cases, or that our concern is misplaced. In Parfit's terms, we usually 'appeal to the interests of those whom our acts affect.' He describes this principle as: '*The Person Affecting Principle, or PAP*: It is bad if people are affected for the worse'. But just because the PAP fails to apply to cases with reproductive effects and negative quality-of-life effects does not mean that there is no appropriate principle that does. It would be fallacious to conclude that because the PAP fails, there is no (X).

Third, we can still engage in a discussion of what precautionary principles we might employ should any actual cloned children come into existence. In other words, even if Parfit's non-identity problem voids appeals to the interests of future children as an argument for prohibiting cloning, it does not apply to appeals to the interests of actual cloned children. Since we are aware that this may become a problem for any children who are cloned, we should be prepared to protect their right to self-determination. Having a complete and healthy ethical discussion now may ensure that suitable policies are ready at the appropriate time, should it ever become necessary. Then, once there are actual cloned children, we will have the normal grounds for applying the PAP and can immediately act to protect them by putting the previously discussed policies into place. The PAP alone can still provide us with the usual reasons for why, given that they have been born, we ought to monitor cloned children for potential psychological harms and safeguard their right to self-determination, which may be more prone to violation than usual.

So, Parfit's non-identity problem shows that it is not quite right to talk about a child being harmed by the act of cloning, because it would not exist otherwise. Parfit thinks that this indicates the need for a different principle than usual—(X) instead of the PAP—but that the moral objection to psychological harming of cloned children remains strong. Certainly, Parfit's non-identity problem does not refute the possibility of an appropriate principle (X)—it only shows that our usual one, the PAP, fails to apply in these cases. Finally, even appealing only to the PAP, Parfit's non-identity problem does not allow for a cursory dismissal of all concern with psychological harms. We still have a responsibility to protect the interests of actual future children who are cloned and may be mistreated. . . .

Balancing Principles in Practice

I hope that this [viewpoint] has shown that there are two distinct claims on liberty in the case of human reproductive cloning: the parents' right to reproductive freedom, and the clones' right to self-determination. Some have tried to dismiss the threat of psychological harms to clones on the grounds that to mistake genetic identity for personal identity is to commit a fallacy and that calling such violations harm incurs Parfit's non-identity problem. But neither claim justifies neglecting the clones' rights in favor of their parents' [rights]. In no case is it acceptable to ignore potential harms simply because they result from a mistake in reasoning. . . . If cloning were to occur, there would be actual children with the right to self-determination that ought to be protected as arduously as this right is protected in children produced in the more usual ways. The terms and extent of this protection are morally relevant to the discussion of human reproductive cloning and ought to be explored rather than ignored.

Periodical and Internet Sources Bibliography

The following articles have been selected to supplement the diverse views presented in this chapter.

Philip Ball	"Frankenstein Syndrome: Why Do We Fear Making Humans?," *New Scientist*, February 11, 2011.
Charles Q. Choi	"Cloning of a Human," *Scientific American*, June 2010.
Katrien Devolder	"Complicity in Stem Cell Research: The Case of Induced Pluripotent Stem Cells," *Human Reproduction*, July 19, 2010.
Muriel Lederman	"The Genomic Revolution: Secrets of Life, Secrets of Death," *Feminist Formations*, Summer 2010.
Jessica Lin Lewis	"Predicting the Judicial Response to an Asserted Right to Reproductive Cloning," *Journal of Legal Medicine*, October–December, 2008.
Michelle N. Meyer	"Throwing the Baby Out with the Amniotic Fluid," *Science Progress*, May 2009. http://scienceprogress.org.
Chris Mason	"Making People: Today's Wariness of Reproductive Technologies Stems from Myths, Legends and Hollywood," *Nature*, March 17, 2011.
Colin Nickerson	"Scientists Say They Cloned Human Embryo," *Boston Globe*, January 18, 2008.
Pia de Solenni	"The Strange World of Assisted Reproductive Technology," LifeNews.com, October 17, 2011. www.lifenews.com.

What Ethical and Moral Issues Surround Animal Cloning?

Chapter Preface

Many people in the world of horse racing would love to see another Secretariat race again. Secretariat was a US Triple Crown champion in 1973. He holds records for the fastest time in the Kentucky Derby and the Belmont Stakes, has been honored with a US postage stamp, and was listed by ESPN as number thirty-five of the one hundred greatest athletes of all time. Secretariat's DNA is only available today in the cells of his descendants, many of whom carry the horse's signature red color and white socks. However, if someone in 1973 had saved some of Secretariat's cells or tissues, it could have been possible for a clone of Secretariat to run in horse races again. Animal cloning has entered the world of horse racing and other equestrian sports. Many people are excited to clone their favorite or most successful horse. However, others think horse cloning is unethical.

An Italian Haflinger foal named Prometea was the first cloned horse. Prometea was born on May 28, 2003, just a few weeks after the first cloned equine, a mule named Idaho Gem. Prometea was cloned from the same mare that carried her to term. In addition to Prometea, the Italian scientists who cloned her cloned about three hundred other embryos. However, Prometea was the only embryo that was viable and survived to term. Prometea is named for Prometheus (Prometeo in Italian), a mythological Greek Titan who stole fire from Zeus and gave it to mortals. According to Cesare Galli, one of the scientists who created Prometea, "She is like the Greek Titan, because she challenged the establishment and the current way of thinking."[1]

Many more horses have been cloned since Prometea's debut in 2003. According to an article in the *Practical Horseman* by Jeannie Blancq Putney, as of January 2011, there were seventy-five cloned horses. Putney's article begins by describing a grand prix horse racer's longing to see his aging 18-year-old horse Sapphire compete at top form again. According to Mark Watring, Sapphire's owner, "Every rider has that special horse—the one they've had success on and built a special bond with . . . so you've got that 28-year-old winner out in the field, and when you look at him, you can't help but wonder, what if we could do that again?" Since Sapphire is a gelding (a castrated male horse), Mark thought he could only dream about the younger version of Sapphire. However, cloning provided a way for Mark's dream to come true. In February 2010, Sapphire's clone—Saphir—was born. "I'm ready to ride him already," Mark told Putney. "I'm very excited about it and what the future may hold."[2]

Many other people in the equestrian world feel as Mark does. Championship polo horses, cutting horses, jumping horses, rodeo horses, and racing mules have all been cloned. Most of those cloned have been geldings. In 2003, just before Prometea and Idaho Gem were born, Don Jacklin, president of the American Mule Racing Association, summed up the lure of cloning to the equestrian world in an article in *New Scientist*. According to Jacklin, "cloning will offer racing enthusiasts an opportunity that will be hard to resist: the chance to perpetuate the lineage of prizewinning horses that have been castrated."[3] Despite the enthusiasm of those like Watring and Jacklin, many people oppose horse cloning. They worry that cloning will lead to the dominance of certain bloodlines, reduce genetic diversity, and weaken the breed. Many traditional horse breeders are among those that do not like cloning. Carol Harris has been breeding horses for sixty years in Florida. In 2010 she told the *Washington Post*'s Stephen Hudak that those who promote horse cloning "smell money" and are "looking for a shortcut to a great horse." According to Harris, "breeding is an art," while "cloning is just replication." Wayne Pacelle, president of the Humane Society of the United States, agrees with Harris. He told Hudak, "the cloning advocates and practitioners are thinking of horses as a commodity. Those on my side of the fence think of horses as individual creatures who deserve respect and humane treatment."[4]

Maggie LeClair, a horse enthusiast and administrative assistant to the dean of the College of Sciences at the University of Central Florida, wrote a letter that appeared in the July 2009 issue of *Florida Equestrian* magazine. According to LeClair, she thought about cloning her beloved horse Cappy. However, she decided against it for ethical reasons. She noted that there are so many horses that are being abandoned and that need loving homes. "Why would anyone clone a horse?" she asked. According to LeClair, "I am not in favor of cloning horses—after all, Cappy was 'One of a Kind.'"[5]

While horses are being cloned to bring back cherished champions, other animals are also being cloned for a variety of reasons. Farm animals are being cloned for food production, zoos are cloning endangered species, and people are cloning their favorite dogs and cats.

Some people are excited about the opportunities animal cloning provides, while others are ethically concerned about the practice. In the following chapter of *Opposing Viewpoints: Cloning*, the authors discuss the many ethical and moral concerns associated with animal cloning.

Notes

1. Nancy Touchette, "Cloned Horse Foal Beats the Odds," Genome News Network, August 7, 2003. www.genomenews network.org.
2. Jeannie Blancq Putney, "The Horse Cloning Conundrum," *Practical Horseman*, January 2011.
3. Sylvia Pagan Westphal, "Horse Cloners Bet Racing Ban Won't Last Long," *New Scientist*, June 7, 2003.
4. Stephen Hudak, "Cloning of Horses Prompts Debate over Registering Genetic Duplicates," *Washington Post*, May 4, 2010.
5. Maggie LeClair, "August Opinions: Horse Cloning," *Florida Equestrian*, July 20, 2009.

"Clones are the 'rock stars' of the barn- yard and therefore are treated like royalty."

Cloning Farm Animals Is Ethical

Biotechnology Industry Organization

In the following viewpoint, the Biotechnology Industry Organi- zation (BIO) contends that animal cloning is ethical. According to BIO, cloning does not cause farm animals to suffer and can even reduce animal suffering by helping to improve an animal's overall health. Continuing improvements in cloning techniques since 1996, when Dolly the sheep was cloned, have made animal cloning safer for the animals, says BIO. The organization con- tends that animal cloning is ethical according to Catholic, Jew- ish, and Muslim thinkers. The Biotechnology Industry Organiza- tion is a trade group of businesses involved in the research and development of health care, agricultural, industrial, and envi- ronmental biotechnology products.

As you read, consider the following questions:

1. According to BIO, what was the finding of a National Academy of Sciences review on the health of cloned ani- mals?

2. According to BIO, what is the only thing in clones that shows any difference from conventional animals when it comes to deformity rates?

3. According to BIO, how did Dolly the cloned sheep die?

What is animal cloning?

Cloning is an assisted reproductive technology that allows livestock breeders to create identical twins of their best animals. This breeding technique does not change the genetic makeup of the animal. The most common procedure used today is known as somatic cell nuclear transfer (SCNT), which makes it possible to produce many animals from a single donor. SCNT involves transferring the genetic information from one animal into an empty oocyte, or egg. This process results in an embryo, which is implanted into a surrogate mother who carries the pregnancy to term.

How does cloning affect the DNA of animals?

Cloning does not change DNA, and clones are not genetically engineered animals. It is simply assisted reproduction, similar to embryo transfer, artificial insemination, or in vitro fertilization.

Is animal cloning a new technology?

Animal cloning has been rigorously studied for decades, since the earliest research on embryo splitting in the late seventies and early eighties. The U.S. Food and Drug Administration has analyzed numerous scientific studies on the subject, conducted over 30 years and encompassing several generations and large families of livestock.

Cloning and Animal Health

Does cloning cause animal suffering?

Cloning enhances animal well-being, and is no more invasive than other accepted forms of assisted reproduction such as in vitro fertilization. In fact, clones are the "rock stars" of the barnyard, and therefore are treated like royalty. Breeding the best possible stock improves the overall health and disease resistance of animal populations. Additionally, because these breeding techniques can improve the overall health and disease resistance of an animal, cloning will greatly reduce animal suffering.

Are animal clones healthy?

Decades of research have shown that cloned animals are as healthy as conventional animals. A National Academy of Sciences (NAS) review found "the health and well-being of somatic cell clones approximated those of normal individuals as they advance into the juvenile stage. Somatic cell cloned cattle reportedly were physiologically, immunologically, and behaviorally normal."

How does the neonatal mortality rate of animal clones compare to other animals?

Any animal conceived through any assisted reproductive technique—AI [artificial insemination], embryo transfer, etc.—has a slightly higher risk of neonatal death. In the hands of skilled scientists, the neonatal death rate of cloned animals approaches that of animals produced by in vitro fertilization. Within hours or days of birth, there are no health differences between clones and non-clones, according to an NAS review panel. A common misconception is that clones suffer a higher deformity rate than other animals. Only the placentas of clones show any difference from animals born conventionally. In fact, these placental problems occur at similar rates in other assisted breeding techniques, such as in vitro fertilization and embryo transfer. Scientists are working to reduce the impact of placental effects on embryo implantation for a successful pregnancy.

Don't clones suffer a higher rate of deformities than other animals?

No. Only placentas of clones show any difference from animals born the conventional way. However, these placental problems occur at similar rates in fetuses produced through other assisted breeding techniques, such as in vitro fertilization and embryo transfer.

Is there a risk of large offspring syndrome (LOS) among animal clones?

LOS occurs naturally in cattle. It is seen at higher rates with any assisted reproductive technologies and is not a problem caused specifically by cloning.

Are embryos lost while creating clones?

Embryos are lost in any form of reproduction—including sexual reproduction. In the hands of skilled practitioners, cloning success rates approach other forms of assisted reproduction.

How has the cloning process evolved since [cloned sheep] Dolly's birth?

Every step of the cloning procedure has improved in the decade since Dolly's birth [in July 1996]. Continuing improvements have reduced health problems seen in early reports to rates approaching those of other reproductive technologies.

Did cloning affect Dolly's health and lead to her premature death?

Dolly died of cancer resulting from viral pneumonia. This disease outbreak killed many other sheep the same year she died [in 2003] and affected many animals housed in the same barn. Although it was widely reported in the press that Dolly suffered from arthritis and may have aged prematurely, there is no evidence in the scientific literature that this was true for Dolly or other clones.

Is cloning ethical?

While it is up to each individual to determine their viewpoint on different technologies, the major world religions do not have an issue with livestock cloning. The Catholic Church, in its "Reflections on Cloning," says "there is a place for research, including cloning, in the vegetable and animal kingdoms." On the whole, leading Muslim and Jewish thinkers also agree that cloning is acceptable to meet standards of kosher and halal.

> "The death and deformities found among many cloned and genetically engineered species appear to be the norm rather than the exception, resulting in needless animal suffering."

Cloning Causes Farm Animals to Suffer

Humane Society of the United States

In the following viewpoint, the Humane Society of the United States (HSUS) contends that cloning is detrimental to animal welfare. The HSUS provides information from several studies documenting high failure rates of the cloning process and high rates of death and abnormalities in cloned animals. Additionally, says the HSUS, the welfare of the surrogate mothers used to birth cloned animals is threatened. According to HSUS, there is a lack of federal oversight concerning the welfare of farm animals, and the agricultural industry is all too willing to sacrifice animal welfare for the sake of profit. The Humane Society of the United States is a nonprofit organization that works to reduce suffering and improve the lives of all animals.

As you read, consider the following questions:

1. According to HSUS, researchers are genetically engineering and cloning farm animals for the food supply for reasons such as what?

2. According to HSUS, a 2003 review of cloning found what survival rate for cloned calves?

3. According to HSUS, does the Animal Welfare Act cover farm animals?

Both the genetic engineering and cloning of animals involve the artificial manipulation of deoxyribonucleic acid (DNA).

Genetic engineering involves the alteration of an animal's genetic information, including the addition (or "knock-in") and the removal or inactivation ("knock-out") of genes or their control sequences. For example, the process of adding a growth hormone gene to increase growth rates starts with isolating the gene, cloning it in bacteria to produce large quantities, and then injecting the gene under a microscope into a pronucleus of an embryo flushed from his or her mother's oviduct. This embryo is then implanted into a surrogate mother who will give birth to offspring, some of whom will be transgenic—that is, containing the exogenous growth hormone gene in all of their cells.

Clones are nearly exact genetic copies of an individual animal. A recipient cell, usually an egg, is enucleated (nearly all of its genetic information is removed), and the nucleus of a cell from the animal to be cloned (the donor animal) is inserted or fused inside the cell. Embryos produced by this nuclear transfer are then cultured in vitro for several cell divisions before being implanted into a surrogate mother. The first mammal successfully cloned from an adult cell, a sheep called Dolly, was born in 1996.

Researchers are genetically engineering and cloning farm animals for the food supply for a number of reasons, such as more profitable muscling and disease resistance. However, many applications of these technologies have been shown to be detrimental to animal welfare.

Genetic Engineering and Animal Welfare

While genetically engineering farm animals to increase bone strength or reduce reception to pain, for example, may improve animal well-being, the broad use of such technology would be unlikely to result in a reduction of suffering. Gene insertion techniques have limited success, as inserted genes may fail to properly reach target cells and may finish in cells of unintended organs. Many embryos develop abnormally and die in utero, while others may be infertile or born with developmental defects, some of which are attributable to these so-called insertional problems.

Still other health issues may not become apparent until later in life. Transgenic animals often exhibit variable or uncontrolled expression of the inserted gene, resulting in illness and death. In one study, ten transgenic piglets were followed from birth through puberty. Half of the animals died or had to be euthanized due to severe health problems during the investigation, indicating a high mortality rate among genetically engineered piglets. In addition, three of the surviving piglets showed decreased cardiac output.

The genetic modification of sheep containing an extra copy of a growth hormone gene resulted in animals who reportedly grew faster, leaner, and larger than those conventionally bred; produced more wool; or produced milk for prolonged periods. Developing more economically profitable sheep reportedly resulted in negative welfare side effects from the excess growth hormone, including increased incidences of diabetes and susceptibility to parasites.

The transgenic "Beltsville pigs" had human growth hormone genes inserted in their genomes with the goal of increasing the animals' productivity. While that was partially achieved, the genetically modified animals reportedly suffered from numerous problems that severely compromised their welfare, including arthritis, diarrhea, lameness, mammary development in males, disruption of estrous cycles, skin and eye problems, loss of libido, lethargy, pneumonia, pericarditis (inflammation of the sac surrounding the heart), and peptic ulcers. Of the 19 pigs expressing the transgene, 17 reportedly died within the first year.

Similarly, a research effort led by U.S. Department of Agriculture (USDA) scientists modified the genes of dairy cows so the animals would be more resistant to mastitis, an inflammation of the udder. Of 330 attempts, only 8 calves were born alive, and of those 8 animals, only 5 survived to adulthood.

Cloning and Animal Welfare

Cloning research also reveals abnormalities and high failure rates, problems widely acknowledged by scientists in the field and potentially indicative of poor animal welfare. Seemingly healthy bioengineered animals are at risk for a variety of defects. "All cloned babies have some sort of errors," cloning pioneer Ryuzo Yanagimachi reportedly claimed. "I'm surprised they can survive it." The list of problems from which clones have suffered is extensive, including diabetes; enlarged tongues; malformed faces; intestinal blockages; shortened tendons; deformed feet; weakened immune systems; respiratory distress; circulatory problems; and dysfunctional hearts, brains, livers, and kidneys.

A 2003 review of cloning procedures found that while hundreds of calves have been cloned worldwide, less than 5% of all cloned embryos transferred into recipient cows have survived, and the majority of the 95% who did not survive died at various stages of development from a predictable pattern of placental and fetal abnormalities. "The low efficiency seriously limits commercial applicability and ethical acceptance of somatic cloning," wrote the scientists, "and enforces the development of improved cloning methods."

Two years later, a review further identifying the challenges of cloning farm animals continued to note a high failure rate:

> "[A]t present it is an inefficient process: in cattle, only around 6% of the embryos transferred to the reproductive tracts of recipient cows result in healthy, long-term surviving clones. Of concern are the high losses throughout gestation, during birth and in the postnatal period through to adulthood. Many of the pregnancy losses relate to failure of the placenta to develop and function correctly. Placental dysfunction may also have an adverse influence on postnatal health."

Upon review of the world's cloned animals, Ian Wilmut, who led the team to clone Dolly the sheep, also reportedly found low success rates and a host of problems such as fetal overgrowth, or large offspring syndrome, in cattle and sheep; heart defects in pigs; developmental difficulties, lung problems, and malfunctioning immune systems in cows, sheep, and pigs; and individual problems, including a lamb barely able to breathe due to grossly thickened muscles surrounding the lungs. He is quoted as saying: "The widespread problems associated with clones has [*sic*] led to questions as to whether any clone was entirely normal. . . . There is abundant evidence that cloning can and does go wrong. . . ."

The U.S. National Academy of Sciences acknowledged many of these problems in its 2002 report, "Animal Biotechnology: Science-Based Concerns," and the U.S. Food and Drug Administration (FDA) also identified these issues during an earlier hearing on cloning. Kathryn Zoon, director of the FDA Center for Biologics Evaluation and Research, testified before Congress that the failure rate remains extremely high for cloned animals. Furthermore, Zoon testified that "when live births occurred there have been deaths and major abnormalities such as defective hearts, lungs and immune systems in the newborns and older animals. In addition, significant maternal safety risks including deaths have been observed."

Despite the high level of inefficiency and recognized animal welfare concerns, the FDA's draft executive summary, "Animal Cloning: A Risk Assessment," claimed that "the proportion of live, normal births appears to be increasing." Members of the FDA's own Veterinary Medicine Advisory Committee, however, reportedly felt that the FDA had not properly characterized the risk to animals and were uneasy about the level of animal suffering a large cloning industry might cause. In 2005, an FDA representative reportedly acknowledged that cloned animals were indeed more likely to suffer birth defects and health problems when very young. Likewise, an article published in 2007 by FDA researchers noted "that perinatal calf and lamb clones have an increased risk of death and birth defects," demonstrating these problems had not been resolved.

A large-scale study of cloned sheep was published in 2006. Out of 93 initial attempts, only 12 clones reached full-term development. Of these 12, 3 lambs were delivered stillborn, 5 died of liver and kidney abnormalities within 24 hours of delivery by caesarian section, 2 died one day after birth from respiratory distress syndrome, and the remaining 2 lambs died at approximately four weeks due to a bacterial complication.

Cloning also threatens the welfare of surrogate mothers. According to the 2001 congressional testimony of Mark Westhusin, director of the Reproductive Sciences Laboratory at Texas A&M University's College of Veterinary Medicine, of the cloned calves who survived after 35 days of gestation, most exhibited placental abnormalities that pose serious health risks not only to the developing fetus and offspring, but also to the surrogate mothers carrying the pregnancies, and have resulted in the deaths of both the fetuses and the surrogate mothers. In addition, the birth weight of cloned calves may be 25%

heavier than normal. Fetal overgrowth, common to sheep and cattle clones, generally necessitates a caesarian section for the surrogates, an invasive surgery which, along with other intrusive reproductive procedures, may be performed repeatedly on the same animal.

A Texas A&M University study of cloned transgenic calves resulted in four surrogate cows dying. Of the 13 fetuses studied, 4 were stillborn and 2 died after birth. One calf was diagnosed with neonatal respiratory distress at birth, only to die four days later. A necropsy revealed that the calf suffered from severe abnormalities: The animal's lungs had never properly developed, the heart was enlarged, and the liver was grossly abnormal. Michael Bishop, past president of former biotechnology company Infigen, is reported as saying such deaths still happen despite improvements in cloning. "We sacrifice the cow and the clone," he stated in a 2001 interview with *New Scientist*. "[A]ll the heroics in the world can't rescue those animals."

Long-Term Welfare Problems

Biotechnology has produced animals with a range of gross deformities. So-called "legless mice," resulted from foreign DNA being inserted into the mice's chromosomes in a manner that altered an endogenous gene, resulting in a mutation. The first generation of mice produced by this procedure, known as insertional mutagenesis, appeared normal. However, when the transgenic mice were interbred, their progeny suffered severe abnormalities, including the loss of limbs, craniofacial malformations such as a cleft lip or cleft palate, and brain anomalies including highly aberrant or missing olfactory lobes. None of the mice survived for more than 24 hours after birth.

Some abnormalities may not show up until later in life. Rudolf Jaenisch, a founding member of the Massachusetts Institute of Technology Whitehead Institute for Biomedical Research, was quoted as stating that "[c]loned animals that reach

Clarifying the Moral Permissibility of Animal Biotechnology

In the decade following the cloning of Dolly the sheep in 1996, the science of animal biotechnology has made steady—even remarkable—progress, but the public's comfort with these new technologies has not increased. Although more than half of the public is opposed to this research, there is very little active dialogue between the proponents of this science and the critics. One explanation for the absence of a robust debate is the challenge of articulating the public's opposition in a form that does not simply reduce to a pure emotivist reaction, which is quickly dismissed by the proponents as parochial or naive. Attempts to give a substantive critique have faced difficult objections from the advocates of this science. On the other side of this fledgling dialogue is not so much an articulated pro-animal biotech position but an attack on the anti-biotech arguments that lays bare the difficulty of capturing theoretically the ethical problems with many of the projects of this new science. But in the absence of compelling arguments critiquing biotechnology, or at least certain parts of it, the net result is a presumption in favor of it. Most worrisome about the state of this debate is what is being implicitly condoned. Having no effective argument to rein in animal biotechnology or distinguish the moral permissibility of various projects, we are tacitly permitting all of them.

Autumn Fiester,
"Justifying a Presumption of Restraint in Animal Biotechnology Research," American Journal of Bioethics, *June 2008.*

birth or beyond may appear normal, but our research shows they're not." "From what we know, I would argue that cloned animals cannot be normal," Jaenisch reportedly concluded. "They can be closer to normal, but not normal."

According to leading cloning scientist David Norman Wells, the development of musculoskeletal problems, such as chronic lameness and severely contracted flexor tendons, in these high-production animals "emphasizes the point that any underlying frailties in cloned animals may not be fully revealed until the animals are stressed in some manner." Wells et al. found that the most common cause of death of cattle they cloned were late-developing musculoskeletal problems so severe that the cows needed to be euthanized.

Immune deficiency may be another defect challenging cloned animals. Researchers with the USDA and the University of Missouri found the immune systems of cloned pigs produced lower levels of cytokines, which are necessary to fight infections. This impaired immune function may contribute to cloned animals' susceptibility to illness and early death. Combined with the decrease in genetic diversity that would necessarily follow from the large-scale adoption of cloning, this technology may have the potential to exacerbate the already serious problem of transboundary epizootics.

Mounting evidence shows that the death and deformities found among many cloned and genetically engineered species appear to be the norm rather than the exception, resulting in needless animal suffering.

Lack of Oversight

The federal Animal Welfare Act does not cover farm animals used in food and fiber research. The lack of regulatory or legal constraints on what can be done to animals in pursuit of increasing agricultural output, coupled with the historical willingness of industrialized agriculture to sacrifice animal welfare for productivity and profit, reveal many of the problems with much biotechnological animal research.

While the FDA is charged with regulating genetically engineered farm animals destined for the food supply under the New Animal Drug Applications (NADA) process, it has not yet developed regulations or public guidance that provide a clear determination of how the NADA process will apply to these animals. As NADAs are confidential by law, there may be no opportunity for prior public review of applications. The regulation of cloned animals is also under the FDA's jurisdiction.

On September 19, 2005, four days before his resignation, former FDA commissioner Lester Crawford explained its position:

> "With respect to use of cloned animals for human food, FDA has stated up front that the risk assessment methodology and all the information used in performing the risk assessment would be publicly available. . . . Until the risk assessment is complete and publicly available, the voluntary moratorium on release of these products into the food supply remains in effect; and secondly, while our risk assessment only addresses the safety of food from animal clones and the risks to the cloned animals, we are well aware that there are many social and ethical issues related to the cloning of animals."

The agency denied a petition filed by a number of organizations, including the Center for Food Safety, Consumer Federation of America, and the Humane Society of the United States in October 2006, seeking regulation of cloned animals. Responding to one of the requests in the petition, which asked that an advisory committee be created to address ethical issues, the FDA's deputy commissioner for policy wrote: "We do not believe we are required . . . to establish an advisory committee to consider animal welfare. . . . We note that we have considered the animal health impacts of animal cloning."

> "Cloning could be a useful tool for preserving the genetic material of an endangered species on the verge of extinction."

Animal Cloning Can Save Endangered Species

Steve Connor

In the following viewpoint, Steve Connor contends that cloning could help preserve endangered species. Connor says scientists have already tried to clone some endangered animals, such as the Pyrenean ibex and the gaur. However, the cloning process is still inefficient, and so far, success has been limited. Connor does not think cloning will be the ultimate answer to saving endangered species from extinction. However, he does believe that cloning could be used to help save some animals on the brink of extinction. Steve Connor is a science writer for the Independent, *a British national newspaper.*

As you read, consider the following questions:

1. What was the big difference between the technique used to clone Dolly the sheep and the process used to clone Celia the bucardo, according to Connor?

2. According to Connor, how many serious projects are investigating the possible use of cloning to preserve threatened species? What are the animals that are being considered for cloning in these projects?

3. According to Connor, what are the biggest threats to wild animals today?

An extinct species of mountain goat called the Pyrenean ibex, or bucardo, has been "resurrected" by scientists who had managed to create a clone of it with the help of domestic goats. Unfortunately the resurrection was short-lived as the newborn kid died within minutes of being born owing to breathing difficulties caused by deformed lungs. However, the feat was a first in that no one had previously managed to create a clone of an extinct species.

Cloning Celia, a Pyrenean Ibex

The scientists, led by Jose Folch of the University of Zaragoza in northern Spain, wanted to see if they could in some way preserve the genetic material of the bucardo. They had taken skin cells from the ear of the last bucardo known to have lived, a female they called Celia. The sampling took place in 1999 and Celia was subsequently released. However, in January 2000 she was found dead next to a fallen tree with her skull crushed. Folch and his colleagues had carefully stored Celia's skin cells in liquid nitrogen at about minus 196°C.

Over several years, they undertook a series of cloning experiments involving the transfer of the cell nuclei containing the bucardo's DNA into a batch of "empty" egg cells from domestic goats, a close relative, which had their own nuclear DNA removed. This is the standard way of producing a clone using the "cell nuclear transfer" technique that led to the creation of Dolly the sheep. The one big difference, however, is that in this case the resulting embryos were "hybrids" of goat eggs and bucardo skin cells, and instead of transferring the embryos back into a female bucardo—there were none available—the scientists used domestic goats as surrogate mothers.

Cloning Is Still Inefficient

The cloning process is still very inefficient, even when done between members of the same species. When, in 1996, Dolly was created from the udder cell of a female sheep, it took 277 attempts to produce just one live, healthy offspring—Dolly. This bucardo experiment was even more inefficient, which is to be expected given that it involves fusing cells from different species. An earlier attempt to clone the bucardo ended in failure in 2003, with just two pregnancies from dozens of attempted embryo transfers. Both pregnancies did not get beyond the two-month stage. In the latest attempt, the scientists had created 439 ibex-goat hybrid cloned embryos. Of these, only 57 were deemed suitable for transfer into surrogate goat mothers. And of the seven pregnancies, just one gave birth to a live offspring.

It is well established that cloned animals often suffer from developmental problems. Very often these problems prevent the pregnancy from continuing normally, and sometimes the cloned offspring that do get born suffer health problems that either kill them in the womb or lead to later ailments in life. This is one of the reasons why some biologists are very concerned about the use of cloning to preserve endangered animals.

There is a very new method being developed called induced pluripotent stem (iPS) cells. As the name implies, it is a way of creating embryonic-like cells from ordinary skin cells by tinkering with a handful of genes. But scientists have demonstrated that the embryonic stem cells created by the iPS method can also develop fully in the womb just like ordinary embryos and result in live births.

The aim eventually is to refine the technique so that, for instance, the skin cells of an endangered animal are genetically

Creating a Prehistoric World

The *idea* of ancient DNA and reproductive cloning—as opposed to the actual scientific techniques—has tantalized novelists, science writers, and the public not only with the lure of time travel but also of resurrection. The recent appearance in the popular media of stories on ancient DNA sourced from Neanderthals and woolly mammoths, combined with reports on the use of tissue samples and cloning in attempts to save critically endangered species . . . , raises an irresistible question: What *if* the combination of ancient DNA with assisted reproduction could bring back an extinct species?

Amy Fletcher, "Genuine Fakes,"
Politics and the Life Sciences, *March 2010.*

manipulated in the laboratory to create iPS cells that can then be made into cloned embryos for transfer into the womb of a surrogate mother. A number of groups are looking into this as a possible alternative to Dolly-like cloning for endangered animals.

There is again some evidence that the offspring created by the iPS technique may not be entirely normal. Cloned mice produced by the iPS method, for instance, do not seem to live as long as ordinary mice. This would have to be taken into account before it is used on bigger animals that are rare or endangered.

Cloning Rare Animals

[Scientists] believe that cloning offers another way of preserving the unique genetic identity of a rare species in the body of living animals that could be used for breeding purposes. Some endangered animals are so rare and so difficult to breed in captivity that cloning offers a viable alternative route to continuing the genetic line, especially if surrogate mothers of a closely related, non-threatened species are used.

There are at least half a dozen serious projects to investigate the possible use of cloning to preserve some of the world's most threatened species. The animals being considered range from the giant panda and the Sumatran tiger, to the African bongo antelope and the pygmy hippo.

There have already been clones of endangered animals. The most famous was Noah, a baby gaur, a wild ox-like bovine from Southeast Asia, which was cloned using the eggs and surrogate wombs of domestic cows. Unfortunately, Noah died within the first 48 hours of being born due to an intestinal infection that may have been made worse by the fact that he was a hybrid clone of a gaur and a cow.

More recently, scientists have had more success with the European mouflon, a rare breed of sheep found in Sardinia, Corsica and Cyprus, that was cloned in 2001. In 2003, a separate team of scientists cloned another type of wild cattle called a banteng, using cow eggs and surrogate mother cows. . . .

The biggest threats to wild animals today are habitat loss, human encroachment, poaching, pollution and climate change. Almost everyone involved in the conservation of species would put tackling these problems far higher up the agenda than cloning.

Cloning Is Not a Panacea, but Could Be Useful

Many experts go further and say that cloning is a harmful distraction from the main job of the preservation of the wilderness, which is being lost at an astonishing rate, along with the animals and plants that live there.

However, there is a case that under certain circumstances, and with certain species, cloning could be a useful tool for preserving the genetic material of an endangered species on the verge of extinction.

It could be especially useful for animals whose genetic diversity is already limited or dwindling. But no one who knows about threatened species believes it is the panacea that could curb the mass extinction of animals and plants currently taking place on the earth.

> *"Every failure involves living, breathing, and too often suffering animals. And for what? To replace a pet? To add an attraction to a zoo?"*

Pet Cloning and Endangered Species Cloning Are Terrible Ideas

Pete Shanks

In the following viewpoint, Pete Shanks takes issue with pet cloning and the cloning of endangered species. According to Shanks, pet cloning and endangered species cloning are publicity stunts and excuses for scientists to clone something. Many animals have suffered and died, he says, for these trivial pursuits. According to Shanks, the harm to animals caused by pet and endangered species cloning far outweighs any inconsequential benefits the techniques might provide. Pete Shanks is a writer who is a regular contributor to the Center for Genetics and Society's blog, Biopolitical Times, *and* GeneWatch, *a magazine dedicated to monitoring biotechnology's social, ethical, and environmental consequences. He is also the author of* Human Genetic Engineering: A Guide for Activists, Skeptics, and the Very Perplexed.

As you read, consider the following questions:

1. How many embryos and surrogates were used to produce Snuppy, the cloned Afghan hound, according to Shanks?

2. According to Shanks, how many essays did BioArts receive in its 2008 competition to give away a clone?

3. What does Shanks suggest is the question researchers are trying to answer by cloning endangered species?

Pet cloning is a terrible idea—and, we now know, an extremely unpopular one. Cloning endangered species is equally foolish. Re-creating extinct species is an absurd concept, whose worst extreme is the proposal to remake a Neanderthal. Taken together, they represent a triumph of reckless technological tinkering and of adolescent curiosity over meaningful ethics.

The idea of cloning pets immediately followed the 1997 announcement of the first mammal cloned from a somatic cell. John Sperling, a multibillionaire, was reading about Dolly the sheep when he whimsically wondered if it would be possible to clone his girlfriend's dog, Missy. He delegated the project to his girlfriend's son, Lou Hawthorne, who ran with it for the next decade.

A dozen laboratories are said to have been interested, but the initial contract went to Texas A&M. They estimated that the project might cost a million a year and take five years. Sperling could afford it—and the A&M team got an entrée to the intriguing world of mammalian cloning.

That was a hot new field in the late 1990s, and a lot of scientists wanted to dive in. By July 2002, 50 papers had been published in peer-reviewed scientific journals, describing 68 experiments involving about 45,000 eggs, 552 "live births" that did not live long and 386 surviving clones, of 7 different species. Cattle accounted for almost half of the survivors, and mice for most of the rest, followed by goats, pigs, sheep, a few rabbits and one cat (a side experiment by the A&M team).

Endangered Species

Some of these attempts involved endangered, or at least vulnerable, species. The first publicity went to Advanced Cell Technology (ACT), which took time out from cows to clone a gaur (*Bos gaurus*, a species of wild cattle), which unfortunately died two days after its birth. One of the sheep was of a wild, endangered variety (*Ovis orientalis musimon*, a European mouflon), which was cloned using a surrogate from a closely related domestic sheep, *Ovis aries*. In 2003, a threatened African wildcat was cloned, using a domestic cat surrogate; in the same year, a banteng (another cow) was born. More recently, there have been a couple of gray wolves, and that seems to be the sum total of 'success' so far.

There are a few legitimate environmentalists who think that cloning could be one of the tools used to assist endangered species. But the problems are substantial. Cloning does nothing to improve their environment; it adds no genetic diversity; it requires many surrogates and egg donors, who may be harmed; and it may distract from lower tech but more practical conservation measures.

Some of the people involved in endangered species cloning may have been well-meaning, but publicity was always part of the point. (ACT in particular was chronically short of capital, and developed a reputation for stunts.) Just look at the names given to these clones: Ditteaux for the Louisiana-based wildcat, CC for the domestic cat, Noah for the gaur, and so on. The master of this was Hawthorne, who first dubbed the dog-cloning effort the Missyplicity Project and then set up a company called Genetic Savings and Clone (GSC), to do gene-banking for pets and eventually to sell pet clones at a profit.

Animal and Pet Cloning Opinion Polls

Cloning...	Date	Approve	Disapprove	Other
Pets	Feb 2002	12	84	4
Endangered species	Feb 2002	29	64	7
Extinct species	Feb 2002	20	72	8
Livestock	Feb 2002	23	71	6

Americans strongly disapprove of pet cloning and very consistently oppose animal cloning in general, even to reestablish endangered or revive extinct species.

TAKEN FROM: Center for Genetics and Society, "Animal and Pet Cloning Opinion Polls," June 1, 2011. www.geneticsandsociety.org.

Except that the technology did not work very well. The A&M team never did clone a dog, though there was one still-birth. And the cat was, to Hawthorne, "a disaster" in terms of public relations: She did not look like the genetic donor. In retrospect, the choice of donor was a mistake, since she was calico. This multicolor pattern is caused by the random silencing, in early development, of one of the two X chromosomes in each cell. The result is that a clone might be black and white (like CC), or orange and white, but never a combination of the three, as the donor was.

Enter Hwang Woo-suk

GSC eventually stopped funding Texas A&M's efforts, and began their own, without much success . . . beyond selling a couple of cats. Meanwhile a team at Seoul National University (SNU) led by the soon-to-be-notorious Hwang Woo-suk was working intensively on the dog problem. They had the advantage of access to animals bred for food and the preparation of a local tonic; reportedly they used 5,000 dogs in their experiments. Finally, in 2005, they succeeded in cloning an Afghan hound—after creating 1,095 embryos and transferring them, over the course of two years, into 123 surrogates, which resulted in three pregnancies, one miscarriage, one puppy that died after 22 days, and one success. (Their cute name: Snuppy, for SNU-puppy.)

This triumph of persistence was rapidly overshadowed by the discovery that Hwang had faked some of his work on human embryonic stem cells, embezzled millions of dollars in government funds, and violated laws and ethical guidelines about acquiring women's eggs. He left SNU in disgrace; at the time of writing [in October 2009], he is still awaiting sentencing. In the meantime, he set up his own research establishment, and Hawthorne hired him. GSC had gone bust, but Hawthorne now headed two other companies: BioArts and Encore Pet Services. And eventually, five clones of the original Missy were born—after a decade of work, millions of dollars and who knows how many surrogates and egg donors.

The one peer-reviewed paper to emerge from all this only covers the work of Hwang's team, and is largely devoted to comparing two different embryo activation methods. In the best case, 14 dogs were needed to produce one live clone. That's with essentially unlimited funds and animals, and some of the most skilled technicians available. A 2008 survey article estimated that only 1%–5% of all cloned embryos transferred into surrogates develop into viable offspring. A 2007 paper by mouflon-cloner Pasqualino Loi et al. described the production of living offspring as "phenomenological," which in this context seems to be a highfalutin, grandiose way of saying that the process is "trial and mostly error."

"Error" is in fact too bland a word. Some animals grow too large in the womb, sometimes to the point of killing their surrogate mothers. Some seem to be developing normally but then are miscarried or stillborn. Some are born unable to breathe, or with skeletal malformations. Some seem healthy at first but rapidly show such signs of discomfort that they have to be killed before they die in agony.

Extinct Species

Despite this, and despite the overall lack of success in cloning endangered species, there has been at least one serious attempt to re-create an extinct one. This was a Pyrenean goat called a bucardo. The last bucardo died in 2000, but tissue samples were saved. In January 2009, there were actually headlines claiming success, even though the kid was unable to breathe and died within minutes.

Several other species have been discussed for re-creation, including the saber-toothed tiger, the short-faced bear, the giant ground sloth, the moa, the Irish elk and the giant beaver. The one that has attracted most attention is the woolly mammoth. Both Hwang and a Japanese team tried and completely failed, because the frozen tissues were too degraded, but now hopeful scientists are estimating that it could be done for $10 million or so.

Here's the plan. First scientists must finish sequencing mammoth DNA, which seems to be less than 1% different from an elephant's (about 400,000 gene variants). Then they take an elephant cell, reprogram it to an embryonic state, and modify it to match the mammoth's sequence. This could then be the basis of a mammoth clone in an elephant's egg, which would be brought to term in an elephant surrogate. That is, if they can find one. Elephants are themselves threatened, but this does not seem to stop the speculation.

Even if all this is possible, which is not certain, it is not entirely clear what the result would be. Genetically, it would be a mammoth, at least essentially. (It would presumably include a tiny bit of elephant mitochondrial DNA, and it seems inevitable that there will be gaps in the code, bridged with stretches of elephant DNA.) But it would surely be one disturbed beast, even if it were physically healthy. There would be no herd, so the social aspect would be lacking, or severely distorted; the vegetation, climate and entire ecological surroundings would be quite different from that of 5–30,000 years ago; it would be a mammoth-like simulacrum.

An even more disturbing prospect has been mooted: cloning a Neanderthal through a similar process. The obvious surrogate would be human, but that's off the table. Instead, the idea would be to modify a chimpanzee, which is genomically very similar to both humans and Neanderthals. Then a chimpanzee surrogate would bring the near-Neanderthal to term. "The big issue," George Church of Harvard has said, "would be whether enough people felt that a chimp-Neanderthal hybrid would be acceptable, and that would be broadly discussed before anyone started to work on it."

The Dog Business

The nascent dog cloning business was rocked by two announcements in the late summer of 2009. First, a Korean company, RNL Bio, announced a major investment in it, with the expressed intention of dropping the price to $30,000. Second, Hawthorne quit. His company, BioArts, had been trying to sell the service at $138,500, and the price-cutting announcement seems to have been the last straw.

Hawthorne seems to think that RNL just wanted to drive him out of business, perhaps because they were involved in litigation over cloning patents. His envoi was a 3200-word statement that revealed, among other things, just how few people want cloned pets. BioArts ran a well-publicized essay competition in 2008 to give away a clone. They expected hundreds of thousands of applications, and received 237.

Opinion polls always suggested animal cloning was unpopular, and this confirmed it. Evidently people understand the absurdity of trying to clone a once-beloved pet. Clones are not copies, and the attempt to make them causes obvious harm to animals. Hawthorne has now admitted that not only did some cloned dogs have unexpected coloration, some had skeletal malformations, and (weirdest of all) one clone of a male was actually born female, presumably because something very strange happened in early development.

Quite exactly what RNL Bio expects from the market is not clear. Until now, they have been using the SNU team, now led by Hwang's former colleague Lee Byeong-chun, who cloned a "drug-sniffing" dog that works for Korean Customs for them; the seven puppies cost over $700,000, which may be too much for the government. (When announced, they all had the same cute name: Toppy, for Tomorrow's Puppy.) There has been discussion of cloning endangered wolves and "a new breed of dogs known for their talent at detecting cancer cells."

None of these seem like much more than publicity stunts. RNL is an ambitious multinational with a major focus on human stem cell treatments. Their president has talked about making human-dog hybrids for medical research, which might give them a reason to develop cloning technologies. The pets, however, seem like a sideshow.

Cloning for Fun

In 1997, it was surprising that somatic cloning worked at all. A decade on, it seems that there has been more to learn from its failures than its successes. In any case, the basic science of developmental biology should not be driven by technological whim.

The very idea of cloning seems to fascinate some scientists, however, and to drive them to find excuses to pursue it. Consider the work on endangered species: What is the question here that researchers are trying to answer? From the outside, it appears to be not so much "How can we help endangered species?" as "How can we use cloning?"

This enthusiasm has survived the failure of the technique to develop as once expected. Efficiency has improved a little, but not much. Every failure involves living, breathing and too often suffering animals. And for what? To replace a pet? To add an attraction to a zoo? Animal welfare arguments are tricky enough in medical research, where the justification is human benefit. When the benefits are so trivial, the harm to animals clearly outweighs them.

A deeper—probably unconscious—motivation may be one of control, a desire to mold the natural world into shapes we ourselves imagined. Let's see what a Neanderthal looks like! Wouldn't that be neat? No, it would not. The result would either be a failure or, in the unlikely and unprovable event that it succeeded, an ethical monstrosity—a near-human created for pure curiosity.

Cloning for fun is simply a bad idea.

> "The countless dogs being pumped out of puppy mills are a far bigger problem to the general dog population than the one hundred or so cloned dogs that have been made."

There Are Worse Things than Dog Cloning

Anna Jane Grossman

In the following viewpoint, Anna Jane Grossman asserts that people concerned about the welfare of dogs have bigger things to worry about than cloning, such as the plight of the dogs used for breeding at puppy mills. Grossman says she isn't condoning dog cloning, and she wouldn't clone her own dog. However, she thinks it could be possible that cloned dogs and the surrogates used to give birth to them could be happier than many household pets. Anna Jane Grossman is the author of Obsolete: An Encyclopedia of Once-Common Things Passing Us By. *Her writing has appeared in many publications, including the* New York Times, Washington Post, Elle, New York Magazine, Marie Claire, Salon, *and* Fortune; *she writes the weekly Do This with Your Pet column for ReadyMade.com.*

As you read, consider the following questions:

1. What does Grossman think about the people she discusses in the ReadyMade.com piece?

2. According to Grossman, every day she sees people who express nothing but love for their dogs, but then do what to them?

3. What is the reason that Grossman won't clone her dog, Amos?

At ReadyMade.com [a website for the magazine *Ready-Made*] I wrote [on April 12, 2011] about the trend of dog cloning, which is the subject of an excellent new book by journalist John Woestendiek, *Dog, Inc.*

Cloning is happening on such a small scale right now that it seems premature to argue for or against it. The world doesn't need more dogs, but the countless dogs being pumped out of puppy mills are a far bigger problem to the general dog population than the one hundred or so cloned dogs that have been made. Should we ever run out of puppies, I know some mutts who'd be happy to work at making more. My dog would knock up the laundry bag if I let him.

If I could take all the funds that have gone into dog cloning and redirect each dollar to a good shelter, or to a subsidized spay/neuter program, I would. I also think we should spend less money on war and more money on education, but the House isn't voting on the budget I submitted. Point is, people spend money on all kinds of things that many people think are less important than whatever is important to them—in my case, animal welfare. Fancy cars, jets, plastic surgery. . . . Think of all the money going towards hunting gear and fur farms and any number of other industries that result in the blatant killing of animals. At least cloning is a wasteful practice that results in some kind of new life.

People who are commenting on the article are saying that *ReadyMade* is condoning the practice of cloning. I'm certainly not condoning it, nor is my editor. The only ones who are condoning it are the people who are profiled in the story. Yet I don't judge them as harshly as many of my readers. In this post, I'm hoping to explain why.

I love my dog, Amos, a lot. A lot a lot a lot a lot. Today is Amos's sixth birthday, and it pains me to think that we probably only have another six or so years to spend together. Cloning currently costs about $100,000. But the technology to successfully clone a dog has only existed since 2005; the commercial business of dog cloning is younger than that and the price has dropped by a third in just the last year. It's a safe bet to say that by the time Amos goes to the great dog run in the sky, dog cloning might be the kind of thing one could do on a blogger's salary.

But even if such a thing were affordable, it's not something I would ever do. The people I discuss in the ReadyMade .com piece are the kinds of people who go to extremes. Do I think these people are wacky? Yes. . . . Do I think they are love sick? For sure. Evil? No, not at all. Mainly, I think they are harbingers of a confused era that doesn't lie far ahead.

The cloning process, which involves inserting DNA into a scooped out unfertilized dog egg and then zapping it with electricity and implanting it into a surrogate, is still pretty unwieldy and not at all humane. For every one animal that is cloned in the Korean lab where all this is happening, it's likely that dozens of animals will have to get surgery to get their eggs taken out or put back in—and none of those bitches volunteered for the job. There are also frequently extra clones that pop up when only one was wanted, and some of these poor souls are languishing in cages while their twins lead more normal doggie lives. In his book, Woestendiek explains that the dog cloning attempts at Texas A&M were ultimately aborted because they couldn't figure out how to do it while also treating the animals in a way that was deemed humane.

But that's not why I won't clone my dog.

Cloned Dogs May Have Better Lives than Many Other Dogs

Yes, I feel all animals should be treated humanely, but I don't think that rescuing the relatively small number of caged Korean clone mules is going to solve the problem. In fact, they are probably being treated relatively well compared to the dogs that are used for breeding at so-called "puppy mills" throughout the world—dogs that are forced to have ten litters inside cages that they'll never leave alive. There are also many dogs living in research labs throughout the country. Often, they are euthanized when they're no longer needed.

But even those dogs are living better than this world's ga-billion enslaved chickens, cows and pigs. I've never really known a cow, chicken or pig. I have, however, eaten many of them. I try to eat ones that supposedly had a better-than-average life (cows who ate grass instead of corn, chickens that supposedly lived outside of cages). I prefer consuming them when they look as little like their original form as possible. Even so, I often lose my appetite the moment I start to think about the life that the moist brown thing on my plate once led. Even the ones that are treated best are still being raised so that we can kill and eat them. And it's not like there's nothing else out there that we could be eating to sustain ourselves.

The fact is that even most household pets aren't even treated as humanely as we'd like. Every day, I see people who express nothing but love for their dogs but then put a choke collar on them, or leave them home alone for twelve hours at a time or install electric fences. These are effective ways of controlling a dog that is living in a human world, but they are methods that aren't a lot of fun for the dog, especially considering that it wasn't his choice to live in a human-dominated world to begin with. They are housed and fed, yes, but they exist in environments full of punishing situations over which they have little control. The rules they are expected to follow are explained in a language they can't speak; they are often reprimanded for behaving more like dogs than humans. The Korean clone surrogates in their cages are leading less enriched lives, but with so many fewer challenges facing them, it's possible that they're actually happier. And at least none of the humans caring for them are priding themselves on being great dog owners while their pups experience the mental turmoil of wearing a bumble bee costume.

Others are against dog cloning because they feel that it's a crime to go to such lengths to create clones when there are so many shelter dogs that need good homes. This is a good point. But that's not why I won't clone my dog.

The number of dogs that have been cloned in the last six years is just a tiny fraction of the number of dogs that are bred and sold every day; those are industries that cause problems on a much larger scale. Like clones, many of the dogs you'll find at a pet store or at a breeder were created to look a certain way, with little regard to their health. Frequently they are bred in terrible conditions and sold off to people who lose interest once the dogs lose their puppy cuteness. They then wind up in shelters themselves. Most clones, at least, are being made by people who have already shown the ability to care for a dog until the end of its natural life. I'm guessing that the majority of the world's $100,000+ cloned dogs will never see the inside of the SPCA [Society for the Prevention of Cruelty to Animals].

But that's not why I won't clone my dog.

One last reason that I've heard against cloning is that it is unnatural to tinker with evolution. This is a hard point to argue, since humans have already messed with dog evolution to the extent that we have. Using plain old canine sperm and vaginas, we've made dogs that have so many health problems that they can only exist because they have us to perform C-sections and wipe their bums. We've bred them to such extremes that you could almost argue that cloning would at least keep the damage from going any further. We've used cloning to curb change in other living things. New apple trees, for instance, are generally grafted from other apple trees in order to create uniform apples throughout orchards. Every red delicious is a clone of every other red delicious tree. . . .

But that's also not why I won't clone my dog.

Why I Won't Clone My Dog

The reason I won't clone Amos is that he is irreplaceable. Amos is more than just his DNA. He is the result of six years of sharing life with me and the people I love. To re-create him, I'd need to move back into each apartment we've lived in together. I'd need to calculate exactly how many of my tears he's licked, and re-inflict the mental scars I made when I made him wear snow boots. I'd need to make myself 25 again. If I could, then I would.

Amos can only exist now. One day when he is gone, I may love another dog. But it will be a different time and a different love. Clone or not, each animal only has one lifetime. I just feel lucky to be sharing mine with this furry unique specimen sitting at my feet.

Happy Birthday, Amos. May there be many more.

Periodical and Internet Sources Bibliography

The following articles have been selected to supplement the diverse views presented in this chapter.

Chris Adriaanse	"A Clone of My Own," *Chemistry & Industry*, March 21, 2011.
BBC News	"Disgraced S Korean Cloner Hwang Back with Coyote Claim," October 17, 2011.
Amy Fletcher	"Genuine Fakes: Cloning Extinct Species as Science and Spectacle," *Politics and the Life Sciences*, March 2010.
Damien Fletcher	"What's the Beef? All You Need to Know About Cloned Meat," *Mirror*, August 5, 2010.
Brandon Keim	"Cloned Puppies: Sure They're Cute, but at What Cost?," *Wired*, August 19, 2008.
Jonathan D. Moreno	"Why We Need to Be More Accepting of 'Humanized' Lab Animals," *Atlantic*, October 4, 2011.
Jeannie Blancq Putney	"The Cloning Conundrum," *Practical Horseman*, January 2011.
Burt Rutherford	"Consumers and Cloning," *BEEF*, July 1, 2007.
Aaron Saenz	"Four Years After Cloning, Drug-Sniffing Dogs Celebrate Remarkable Success in South Korean Airport," *Singularity Hub* (blog), October 4, 2011. http://singularityhub.com.
Rod Smith	"Cloning to Select Superior Cattle, Hogs as Process May Make Livestock Markets 'Very Different,'" *Feedstuffs*, March 10, 2003.
Rob Waters	"Animal Cloning: The Next Phase," *Bloomberg BusinessWeek*, June 10, 2010.

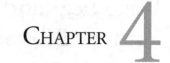

How Should Cloning Be Regulated?

Chapter Preface

On March 8, 2005, the United Nations (UN) General Assembly voted on a contentious international declaration to ban human cloning. The UN Declaration on Human Cloning calls for countries "to prohibit all forms of human cloning inasmuch as they are incompatible with human dignity and the protection of human life." The United States, Germany, Italy, and eighty-one other countries voted to adopt the ban, while the United Kingdom, South Korea, Brazil, and thirty-one other countries voted against it. Thirty-seven countries abstained from the voting. The declaration actually started out as a legally binding convention. However, after an intense debate over whether or not research cloning should be banned, the convention was abandoned and the declaration was adopted.

The 2005 declaration is the second international declaration adopted by the UN to ban human cloning. The UN Universal Declaration on the Human Genome and Human Rights was adopted by the General Assembly on November 11, 1997. The declaration specifically bans human reproductive cloning, but does not refer to research cloning. Article 11 of the declaration states: "Practices which are contrary to human dignity, such as reproductive cloning of human beings, shall not be permitted." This declaration was adopted unanimously and without controversy.

Declarations are a type of legal document that are used by the UN to express the ethics of the international community. They are not legally binding, meaning that governments do not face sanctions for not adhering to them. However, they often exert a political and moral influence on the world. For instance, the UN Universal Declaration of Human Rights, has been an important weapon in the fight against oppression and discrimination around the world.

Conventions, also called treaties or covenants, are another type of legal document used by the UN. Conventions are stronger than declarations. They are binding on the governments that agree to them. UN conventions must be ratified and enacted by the government of each country that agrees to them. The United States is legally bound by several international conventions including the Geneva Conventions and the United Nations convention against torture.

In 2001 the governments of France and Germany submitted a proposal to the UN to begin discussing a convention that would ban human cloning. Diplomats from the two countries felt that a legally enforceable ban on reproductive cloning was urgently needed. An Italian doctor, Severino Antinori, had been making claims that he was going to clone a human baby. Antinori was known in Italy as Dr. Miracle because he helped so many infertile women, including one who was sixty-two years old, conceive children. The French-German proposal to discuss a ban on cloning referred to Antinori and described his cloning plans as "an attack on the dignity of individuals."[1]

As 2001 drew to a close, the UN established a committee to begin drafting the proposed convention. Discussions over its text began in earnest. However, they would go on for several years as disagreements over a single issue emerged.

The discussions revealed that the vast majority of countries endorsed a ban on human reproductive cloning. However, this consensus fell apart when it came to research cloning. One group of countries, including France, Germany, and the United Kingdom, wanted to ban reproductive cloning, but not research cloning. These countries generally did not want to impede stem cell research, and they did not think a consensus could be achieved on research cloning. A second group of countries, lead by the United States and Costa Rica, supported a comprehensive ban on all forms of human cloning, i.e., cloning for reproduction and cloning for research. President George W. Bush weighed in on the issue. Addressing the

United Nations in New York on September 21, 2004, President Bush said, "In this session, the UN will consider a resolution sponsored by Costa Rica calling for a comprehensive ban on human cloning. I support that resolution, and urge all governments to affirm a basic ethical principle: No human life should ever be produced or destroyed for the benefit of another."[2]

The issue of adopting a convention banning human cloning remained on the docket at the UN for three years, while the international community negotiated over whether to ban all cloning or just reproductive cloning. The coalition of countries supporting a ban only on reproductive cloning began weakening. Germany and France moved toward supporting a comprehensive ban. However, the United Kingdom and other countries remained firmly opposed.

Finally, in November 2004, the representative from Morocco offered an alternative. Morocco recommended that the countries draft a declaration against human cloning rather than a convention. The UN Declaration on Human Cloning began to take shape. A vote on the UN Declaration on Human Cloning was taken, on March 8, 2005. It called on its signatory countries to "adopt all measures necessary to protect adequately human life in the application of life sciences" and to "prohibit all forms of human cloning inasmuch as they are incompatible with human dignity and the protection of human life."

The vote was eighty-four for; thirty-four opposed; and thirty-seven abstaining. Among those voting for the ban were the United States, Australia, Costa Rica, and Germany. Those voting against the ban were Belgium, Canada, China, and South Korea. The representative of the United Kingdom said he voted against the declaration, "because the reference to 'human life' could be interpreted as a call for a total ban on all forms of human cloning." He could not accept such an ambiguous declaration, which might sow confusion about the acceptability of that important field of research. The representative of Costa Rica said the adoption of the declaration "constituted a historic step to promote human rights and guarantee human dignity in all circumstances."[3]

The debate surrounding the UN Declaration on Human Cloning illustrates the diversity of ethical and political views about regulating human cloning around the world. Within the United States, there also exists a diversity of views about regulations on cloning. In the following chapter of *Opposing Viewpoints: Cloning*, some of these diverse views are expressed.

Notes

1. Paul Webster and John Hooper, "France and Germany Seek UN Ban on Cloning of Humans," *Guardian*, August 10, 2001.
2. George W. Bush, "Address to the United Nations New York," Presidentialrhetoric.com, September 21, 2004. www.presidentialrhetoric.com.
3. "General Assembly Adopts United Nations Declaration on Human Cloning by Vote of 84-34-37," Press Release GA/10333, UN.org, March 8, 2005. www.un.org.

"We remain the only major nation in the high-tech world that cannot summon itself to ban human cloning."

The United States Should Ban Reproductive Cloning and Place a Moratorium on Research Cloning

Leon R. Kass

In the following viewpoint, written in the political environment of the 2008 elections, Leon R. Kass contends that the time is right to ban reproductive cloning and to put a moratorium on research cloning. Kass says the human cloning debate has gotten entangled with the embryonic stem cell debate and has made it difficult for the US government to effectively ban any human cloning. However, Kass sees the emergence of induced pluripotent stem cell (iPSC) research as being able to change the scientific and political landscape enough that it will be possible to finally ban cloning in the United States. Kass calls for a complete ban on reproductive cloning and a four- or five-year moratorium on research cloning. As of 2012, there are still no federal laws in the United States that ban cloning, although several states have en-

Leon R. Kass, "Defending Life and Dignity: How, Finally, to Ban Human Cloning," *The Weekly Standard*, vol. 13, no. 23, February 25, 2008. Copyright © 2008 by The Weekly Standard. All rights reserved. Reproduced by permission.

acted laws to ban reproductive cloning. *Leon R. Kass is a physician, a professor at the University of Chicago, and the Hertog Fellow at the American Enterprise Institute for Public Policy Research. His books include* Toward a More Natural Science: Biology and Human Affairs *and* Life, Liberty and the Defense of Dignity: The Challenge for Bioethics.

As you read, consider the following questions:

1. With what does Kass say the deepest challenge posed by cloning has to do?

2. Why does Kass believe that the ability to reprogram adult stem cells means that cloning for the purposes of biomedical research has lost its initial reason for being?

3. According to Kass, by addressing separately the cloning and embryo research issues, battles will be fought exactly on the principles involved. What two principles does he describe?

In his [2008] State of the Union address President [George W.] Bush spoke briefly on matters of life and science. He stated his intention to expand funding for new possibilities in medical research, to take full advantage of recent breakthroughs in stem cell research that provide pluripotent stem cells without destroying nascent human life. At the same time, he continued, "we must also ensure that all life is treated with the dignity that it deserves. And so I call on Congress to pass legislation that bans unethical practices such as the buying, selling, patenting, or cloning of human life."

As in his previous State of the Union addresses, the president's call for a ban on human cloning was greeted by considerable applause from both sides of the aisle. But Congress has so far failed to pass any anti-cloning legislation, and unless a new approach is adopted, it will almost certainly fail again.

Fortunately, new developments in stem cell research suggest a route to effective and sensible anti-cloning legislation, exactly at a time when novel success in cloning human embryos makes such legislation urgent. Until now, the cloning debate has been hopelessly entangled with the stem cell debate, where the friends and the enemies of embryonic stem cell research have managed to produce a legislative stalemate on cloning. The new scientific findings make it feasible to disentangle these matters and thus to forge a successful legislative strategy. To see how this can work, we need first to review the past attempts and the reasons they failed.

The Two Sides in the Cloning and Stem Cell Debate

Three important values, differently weighted by the contending sides, were (and are) at issue in the debates about cloning and embryonic stem cells: scientific and medical progress, the sanctity of human life, and human dignity. We seek to cure disease and relieve suffering through vigorous research, conducted within acceptable moral boundaries. We seek to protect vulnerable human life against destruction and exploitation. We seek to defend human procreation against degrading reproductive practices—such as cloning or embryo fusing—that would deny children their due descent from one father and one mother and their right not to be "manufactured."

Embryonic stem cell research pits the first value against the second. Many upholders of the sanctity of human life regard embryo destruction as unethical even if medical good may come of it; many partisans of medical research, denying to nascent human life the same respect they give to life after birth, regard cures for disease as morally imperative even if moral harm may come of it. But the deepest challenge posed by cloning has to do not with saving life or avoiding death, but with human dignity, and the cloning issue is therefore only accidentally bound up with the battle about stem cell research. Yet both parties to the stem cell debate happily turned the cloning controversy into the life controversy.

The faction favoring embryonic stem cell research wanted to clone embryos for biomedical research, and touted cloning's potential to produce individualized (that is, rejection-proof) stem cells that might eventually be used for therapy. Its proposed anti-cloning legislation would ban only "reproductive cloning" (cloning to produce children) while endorsing the creation of cloned human embryos for research. Such cloning-for-biomedical research its proponents originally called "therapeutic cloning," hoping that the goal of "therapy" would get people to overcome their repugnance for "cloning." But when that strategy backfired, they disingenuously denied that the cloning of embryos for research is really cloning (they now call it, after the technique used to clone, SCNT, somatic cell nuclear transfer). They also denied that the product is a human embryo. These Orwellian tactics succeeded in confusing many legislators and the larger public.

The faction opposed to embryonic stem cell research wanted to safeguard nascent human life. Its proposed anti-cloning legislation would ban all human cloning—both for reproduction and for biomedical research—by banning the initial step, the creation of cloned human embryos. (This is the approach I have favored, largely because I thought it the most effective way to prevent the production of cloned children.) But most of the bill's pro-life supporters cared much more that embryos not be created and sacrificed than that children not be clones. Accordingly, they sought to exploit the public's known opposition to cloning babies to gain a beachhead against creating embryos for destructive research, which practice, although ineligible for federal funding, has never been illegal in the United States. Initially, this strategy worked. . . . But momentum was lost in the Senate, owing to delays caused by 9/11 [referring to the September 11, 2001, terrorist attacks on the United States] and strong lobbying by the pro–stem cell forces, after which time an impasse was reached, neither side being able to gain enough votes to close debate.

Sensible Recommendations from the President's Council on Bioethics

Concerned that the United States appeared to be incapable of erecting any moral barriers to the march toward a Brave New World, the President's Council on Bioethics (I was then its chairman) sought to show the president and Congress a way forward. Setting aside our deep divisions (on the moral status of human embryos and federal funding of stem cell research), we successfully sought common ground and recommendations on which we could all agree.

In our 2004 report, "Reproduction and Responsibility," we unanimously proposed a series of legislative bans to defend human procreation against certain egregious practices—practices that would blur the boundary between the human and the animal, exploit the bodies of women, deny children the right to normal biological lineage, and commodify nascent human life. We called for legislative moratoria on: the placement of a human embryo in the body of an animal; the fertilization of a human egg by animal sperm (or vice versa); the transfer of a human embryo to a woman's uterus for purposes other than producing a child; the buying, selling, and patenting of human embryos or fetuses; and (on the cloning front) the conception of a child other than by the union of egg and sperm, both taken from adults—a provision that would ban cloning as well as other unwelcome forms of reproduction.

Though these recommendations received a favorable response from the White House and from some members of Congress (in both parties), our recommendations were attacked from both sides. The scientists and the assisted-reproduction professionals, as anticipated, wanted no restrictive federal legislation whatsoever. Surprisingly, we were hit also from the right: Several leading pro-lifers objected to the "children's provision" on the ground that it appeared to be a retreat from the . . . total ban on cloning—a bill they nevertheless conceded had no chance of passage in the Senate. To my astonishment, some powerful lobbyists privately told me they objected also to the animal-transfer provision, on the grounds that one should not ban any method that might rescue "extra" IVF [in vitro fertilization] embryos that would otherwise die. (When pressed on this point, one interlocutor said that she would gladly give a child a pig for a mother if that were the only way to rescue an otherwise doomed embryo!)

Of the council's sensible recommendations, only one has been enacted: a ban on initiating a pregnancy for any purpose other than to produce a child. (This bill, enacted as an anti-"fetal-farming" rather than a defense of women measure, also amended the existing statute to forbid the use of cells or tissues derived from a human embryo gestated in an animal.)

A New Approach

Fast-forward to 2008. We are in the last year of the Bush presidency. Despite the president's numerous calls for action, we remain the only major nation in the high-tech world that cannot summon itself to ban human cloning, thanks to the standoff over the embryo issues. Fortunately, science has given Congress another chance to act. In the last six months, the scientific landscape has changed dramatically. On the one hand, the need for anti-cloning legislation is now greater than ever; on the other hand, there are reasons why a new approach can succeed.

Here is what's new. After the 2005 Korean reports of the cloning of human embryos turned out to be a fraud, many said that human cloning could not be achieved. Yet late in 2007 Oregon scientists succeeded for the first time in cloning primate embryos and growing them to the blastocyst (5-7 day) stage, and then deriving embryonic stem cells from them.

The Sanctity of Human Life Act

SEC. 3. DEFINITIONS.

For purposes of this Act:

1. FERTILIZATION—The term "fertilization" means the process of a human spermatozoan penetrating the cell membrane of a human oocyte to create a human zygote, a one-celled human embryo, which is a new unique human being.

2. CLONING—The term "cloning" means the process called somatic cell nuclear transfer, which combines an enucleated egg and the nucleus of a somatic cell to make a human embryo.

3. HUMAN; HUMAN BEING—The terms "human" and "human being" include each and every member of the species *Homo sapiens* at all stages of life, beginning with the earliest stage of development, created by the process of fertilization, cloning, or its functional equivalent.

"H.R. 212," 112th Congress 1st Session, January 7, 2011.

More recently, other American scientists, using the Oregon technique, have reported the creation of cloned human embryos. The age of human cloning is here, and the first clones, alas, do not read "made in China."

On the stem cell front, the news is decidedly better. In the last two years, several laboratories have devised methods of obtaining pluripotent human stem cells (the functional equivalent of embryonic stem cells) without the need to destroy embryos. The most remarkable and most promising of these approaches was reported last November by both Japanese and American scientists (including James Thomson, the discoverer of human embryonic stem cells). It is the formation of human (induced) pluripotent stem cells (iPSCs) by means of the reprogramming (also called de-differentiation) of somatic cells. Mature, specialized skin cells have been induced to revert to the pluripotent condition of their originating progenitor.

The therapeutic usefulness of this approach has also been newly demonstrated, by the successful treatment of sickle-cell anemia in mice. Some iPSCs were derived from skin cells of an afflicted mouse; the sickle-cell genetic defect in these iPSCs was corrected; the treated iPSCs were converted into blood-forming stem cells; and the now-normal blood-forming stem cells were transferred back into the afflicted mouse, curing the disease.

Scientists have hailed these results. All parties to the stem cell debates have noted that the embryonic stem cell war may soon be over, inasmuch as science has found a morally unproblematic way to obtain the desired pluripotent cells. But few people have seen the implications of these developments for the cloning debate: Cloning for the purpose of biomedical research has lost its chief scientific raison d'etre [reason for being]. Reprogramming of adult cells provides personalized, rejection-proof stem cells, of known genetic makeup, directly from adults, and more efficiently than would cloning. No need for human eggs, no need to create and destroy cloned embryos, no need for the inefficient process of deriving stem cell colonies from cloned blastocysts. Ian Wilmut himself, the British scientist who cloned Dolly the sheep, has abandoned his research on cloning human embryos to work with reprogrammed adult cells.

Another effect of this breakthrough is that the value for stem cell research of the spare embryos that have accumulated in IVF clinics has diminished considerably, defusing the issue of the ban on federal funding of such research. Why work to derive new stem cell lines from frozen embryos (of unknown quality and unknown genetic composition, and with limited therapeutic potential owing to transplant immunity issues) when one can work with iPSCs to perfect the reprogramming approach and avoid all these difficulties?

Advancing the Positive Aspects of Biomedical Progress

That's not the only way the new scientific landscape changes the policy and legislative pictures. We are now able to disentangle and independently advance all three of the goods we care about. First, it now makes great sense to beef up federal support for regenerative medicine, prominently featuring ramped-up work with iPSCs (and other non-embryo-destroying sources of pluripotent human stem cells). The timing is perfect. The promise is great. The potential medical payoff is enormous. And the force of example for future public policy is clear: If we exercise both our scientific wit and our moral judgment, we can make biomedical progress, within moral boundaries, in ways that all citizens can happily support.

Second, we should call for a legislative ban on all attempts to conceive a child save by the union of egg and sperm (both taken from adults). This would ban human cloning to produce children, but also other egregious forms of baby making that would deny children a link to two biological parents, one male and one female, both adults. . . . It pointedly neither endorses nor restricts creating cloned embryos for research: Cloning embryos for research is no longer of such interest to scientists; therefore, it is also no longer, as a practical matter, so important to the pro-life cause. Moreover, the prohibited deed, operationally, should be the very act of creating the conceptus (with intent to transfer it to a woman for pregnancy), not . . . the transfer of the proscribed conceptus to the woman, a ban that would have made it a federal offense not to destroy the newly created cloned human embryos. The ban proposed here thus deserves the support of all, regardless of their position on embryo research.

Third, the time is also ripe for a separate bill to defend nascent life, by setting up a reasonable boundary in the realm of embryo research. We should call for a (four- or five-year) moratorium on all de novo [new] creation—by whatever means—of human embryos for use in research. This would block the creation of embryos for research not only by cloning (or SCNT), . . . but also by IVF. Such a prohibition can now be defended on practical as well as moral grounds. Many human embryonic stem cell lines exist and are being used in research; 21 such lines, still viable, are available for federally funded research, while an even greater number are being studied using private funds. The new iPSC research, however, suggests that our society can medically afford, at least for the time being, to put aside further creation of new human life merely to serve as a natural resource and research tool. We can now prudently shift the burden of proof to those who say such exploitative and destructive practices are absolutely necessary to seek cures for disease, and we can require more than vague promises and strident claims as grounds for overturning the moratorium.

The Value of the "Triple-Pronged Approach"

Morally and strategically speaking, this triple-pronged approach has much to recommend it. It is at once more principled, more ambitious, and more likely to succeed than its predecessors. By addressing separately the cloning and embryo-research issues, we can fight each battle exactly on the principle involved: defense of human procreation or defense of human life. By broadening the first ban to include more than cloning, we can erect a barrier against all practices that would deny children born with the aid of reproductive technologies the ties enjoyed by children conceived naturally. By extending the second ban to cover all creation of life solely as an experimental tool, we can protect more than merely embryos created by cloning. We would force everyone to vote on the clear principles involved: Legislators would have to vote yea or nay on both weird forms of baby making and the creation of human life solely for research, without bamboozling anyone with terminological sleights of hand. And by combining these legislative restrictions with strong funding initiatives for regenerative medicine, we can show the American people and the world that it is possible to vigorously pursue the cures all dearly want without sacrificing the humanity we rightly cherish.

Politically as well, this triple-pronged approach is a winner for all sides. Because the latest science has made creating embryos for research unnecessary and inefficient by comparison with reprogramming, we have the chance to put stem cell science on a footing that all citizens can endorse. Indeed, in return for accepting a moratorium on a scientific approach that is not very useful (creation of new embryos for research), scientists could exact large sums in public support for an exciting area of science. With pro-lifers as their biggest allies, they could obtain the research dollars they need—and their supposed enemies would write the biggest checks. Meanwhile, at the very time the latest science has made affronts to human procreation—cloning, but not only cloning—more likely and even imminent, pro-lifers and scientists can come together to ban these practices in America, as they have already been banned in the rest of the civilized world, without implicating the research debate at all.

In an election year, Congress will be little moved to act quickly on these seemingly low-priority items. Moreover, the partisans who have produced the current impasse may still prefer to keep things at stalemate, the better to rally their constituents against the other side. But we can ill afford to be complacent. The science is moving very rapidly. Before the end of the summer [2008], we may well hear of the cloning of primate babies or perhaps even of a human child. Now is the time for action, before it is too late.

> *"Banning human cloning sends the regrettable message that politics and public pressure triumph over logic and the law."*

The United States Should Not Ban Human Cloning

Elizabeth Price Foley

In the following viewpoint, Elizabeth Price Foley contends that cloning is protected under the First Amendment of the US Constitution and that using cloning to procreate is a fundamental constitutional right. Foley examines important legal cases and the impact of judicial rulings on cloning. She concludes that First Amendment protections of free speech extend to scientists' right to perform cloning. Additionally, she concludes that the due process clauses of the Constitution protect an individual's right to procreate, including the right to procreate through cloning. Elizabeth Price Foley is a legal theorist who writes and comments in the fields of constitutional law, bioethics, and health care law. She is the Institute for Justice chair in constitutional litigation and professor of law at Florida International University College of Law.

Elizabeth Price Foley, "The Constitutional Implications of Human Cloning," *Arizona Law Review*, vol. 43, no. 2, June 11, 2011, pp. 16–46. Copyright © 2011 by Arizona Law Review. All rights reserved. Reproduced by permission.

As you read, consider the following questions:

1. According to Alexander Meiklejohn, the First Amendment was designed to ensure what?

2. According to Foley, *Skinner* is not a due process case. What kind of case does Foley say it is?

3. According to Foley, in *Lindley*, the court suggests that a critical factor in determining the scope of the fundamental right of procreation is what?

While there is undoubtedly great popular support for banning human cloning both at the federal and state level, there are several possible constitutional impediments to doing so. Even if cloning bans are enacted (as they have already been in several states), such bans likely will be challenged on various constitutional grounds. This section explores the likelihood of success of such challenges.

Cloning Bans Would Likely Violate the First Amendment

The opponents of human cloning do not seem content with a ban on governmental funding of human cloning research, which has already been implemented. Rather, they seek to ban all human cloning research, regardless of whether the research is conducted with public or private dollars. In effect, the current cloning ban proposals would say to scientists, "thou shalt not research" in this particular area.

As an initial matter, it should be noted that a simple ban on federal funding of scientific research is not constitutionally troubling. Congress has the power, pursuant to the spending clause, to spend federal dollars in any way it wishes, so long as the spending can be said to be within the broad notion of the "general welfare." Congress thus has the corresponding constitutional power to deny federal funding of scientific research it deems not in furtherance of the general welfare. The Executive

Branch may likewise restrict federal funding, provided it is not contrary to statutory language. In the mid-1970s, for example, the National Institutes of Health ("NIH") and other federal agencies promulgated regulations restricting federal funding of recombinant DNA research that did not conform to certain guidelines. Likewise, in the 1980s, the Reagan and Bush administrations imposed a fetal tissue research ban, which specified that federal dollars could not be spent on fetal tissue research. The rationale behind the restriction was that federal funding of such research would create a need for fetal tissue, which in turn could encourage more women to have abortions.

The research restrictions on recombinant DNA and fetal tissue were qualitatively different from the proposed federal or state bans on human cloning because they merely restricted public funding of such research and did nothing to prevent such research from being funded by private dollars. The proposed bans on human cloning, by contrast, would prohibit all cloning research or specific applications thereof, whether publicly or privately funded.

The question therefore becomes whether a law banning all cloning research, or specific applications thereof, would run afoul of the First Amendment, which states that "Congress shall make no law . . . abridging the freedom of speech. . . ." It is well accepted, of course, that the First Amendment is not absolute. Even protected speech may be regulated, provided the law in question is necessary to further a compelling governmental interest. It is necessary, therefore, to determine whether scientific research—such as human cloning—constitutes "speech," and, if so, to what extent such speech is protected.

One of the most commonly held views of the Founders' purpose in drafting the First Amendment is that it was designed to ensure robust discussion through protection of the "marketplace of ideas." Another common view is that the First

Amendment is designed to protect speech and expressive conduct which is essential to informed self-governance. Alexander Meiklejohn posits that the First Amendment was designed to ensure the existence of a well-informed citizenry capable of self-governance by protecting such things as education, philosophy, science, literature, and the arts, and public discussions of public issues. He concludes:

> I believe, as a teacher, that the people do need novels and dramas and paintings and poems, "because they will be called upon to vote." The primary social fact which blocks and hinders the success of our experiment in self-government is that our citizens are not educated for self-government. We are terrified by ideas, rather than challenged and stimulated by them. Our dominant mood is not the courage of people who dare to think. It is the timidity of those who fear and hate whenever conventions are questioned.

Thus, the First Amendment protects ideas, not because of their substantive merit but simply because ideas stimulate thought, which in turn breeds the courage and boldness necessary for effective self-governance. And while cloning research is clearly disturbing to many, the Supreme Court has stated that "the First Amendment ordinarily prohibits courts from inquiring into the content of expression, except in cases of obscenity or libel, and protects speech . . . regardless of [its] motivation, orthodoxy, truthfulness, timeliness, or taste. . . ."

Scientific Actions Are Expressions of Ideas

But what of scientific *action*? Can a scientist be punished for action, i.e., for testing certain kinds of hypotheses? After all, once a scientific idea or hypothesis is formed, the scientist naturally wants to test his hypothesis through the scientific method. Any hypothesis untested by research or experimentation is relatively useless. The legislative bans on human cloning enacted thus far do not prohibit anyone from *thinking* about human cloning, but from *acting* upon their thoughts by engaging in certain actions. The proposed federal anti-cloning bills, for example, would prohibit either: (1) all use of somatic cell nuclear transfer techniques; or (2) the implantation into a mother's womb of a human embryo created by cloning. The former would prohibit all scientific experimentation using cloning techniques (whatever the ultimate goal of the scientist may be), whereas the latter would prohibit a scientist from actually implanting a human embryo created by cloning. Both, of course, ban action, not thoughts.

May such scientific action be proscribed consistent with the First Amendment? The Supreme Court has long held that the First Amendment free speech clause protects "expressive conduct," such as the wearing of black armbands in protest of the Vietnam War, the display of an American flag with a superimposed peace symbol, or the refusal of schoolchildren to salute the flag. While almost all speech arguably contains an element of conduct, the court, in *Spence v. Washington*, articulated a two-part test for determining whether conduct is sufficiently expressive as to warrant First Amendment protection: (1) the conduct must be intended to "convey a particularized message"; and (2) there must be a "great" likelihood that "the message would be understood by those who view . . . it."

Would scientific research satisfy the two-pronged test of *Spence v. Washington?* Scientific research and experimentation is undoubtedly intended to "convey a particularized message" about the value and utility of underlying intellectual ideas—an unmistakable message to all who view the resulting scientific data. A scientist conducts experiments to either prove or disprove a hypothesis through the scientific method. Through experimentation, scientists express their creativity and intellectuality in much the same way that musicians express themselves through music or artists express themselves through art. A law which banned scientific research on human cloning could therefore interfere with the conveyance of a message in the same way as would a law which banned impressionistic painting or rap music.

A more narrow legislative ban on certain specific *applications* of human cloning research, such as a ban only on the implantation of the embryo into a womb, could also present First Amendment problems. Under such legislation, the banned conduct—implantation of a human embryo created by cloning into a womb—arguably is "intend[ed] to convey a particularized message" that would have a "great" likelihood of being "understood by those who viewed it." The message being sent by an attempt at implantation would be that "human cloning is normatively worthwhile and technologically possible"—a message with a great likelihood to be understood by most people who viewed or otherwise learned of the attempted implantation.

By attempting implantation, a scientist would be applying the knowledge she has gained from scientific research. Attempting implantation is therefore a natural and logical next step, a step fully as expressive as, for example, performing a play one has written or singing a song one has composed. Absent a compelling interest, the government could no more ban the performing of a play than the writing of it. If human cloning research is expressive conduct protected by the First Amendment, so too should be the actual expression of that research (e.g., implantation). . . .

The Right to Procreate

The due process clauses of the Fifth and Fourteenth Amendments prohibit, respectively, federal or state governments from depriving any individual of "life, liberty, or property without due process of law." These clauses have long been interpreted as not only providing protection against procedural unfairness but also as providing positive, substantive protection against governmental deprivations of life, liberty, or property. . . .

One of the most important cases implying a positive right of procreation is the 1923 decision in *Meyer v. Nebraska*, in which the Supreme Court struck down a Nebraska law which prohibited the teaching of any language other than English to children prior to the eighth grade. Specifically, the court held that the law violated the "liberty" interest protected by the due process clause of the Fourteenth Amendment, stating in dicta [in their opinion]:

Without doubt, [the liberty interest of the due process clause] denotes not merely freedom from bodily restraint but also the right of the individual . . . to marry, establish a home and bring up children . . . and generally to enjoy those privileges long recognized at common law as essential to the orderly pursuit of happiness by free men.

Thus, the liberty interest protected by the Constitution appeared to the court, in 1923, to encompass much more than simply a right to be free from physical restraint; it encompassed affirmative rights to the essentials of individual domestic happiness: marriage, establishment of a home, and the raising of children.

The Supreme Court subsequently and more specifically addressed the right of procreation in the case of *Skinner v. Oklahoma*, in which the court invalidated an Oklahoma statute which mandated sterilization for criminals convicted two or more times for felonies involving moral turpitude. Strictly speaking, *Skinner* is an equal protection clause case, not a due process case. The court invalidated the law in question because it forced sterilization upon certain habitual felons convicted of crimes of "moral turpitude" but left other habitual felons untouched. The court noted the discriminatory effect of the law, stating:

A clerk who appropriates over $20 from his employer's till and a stranger who steals the same amount are thus both guilty of felonies. If the latter repeats his act and is convicted three times, he may be sterilized. But the clerk is not subject to the pains and penalties of the act no matter how large his embezzlements nor how frequent his convictions.

Skinner clearly intimates that procreation is a fundamental right, since the court invoked strict scrutiny, proclaiming that "marriage and procreation are fundamental to the very existence and survival of the [human] race" and concluded that, by preventing conception, the law in question interfered with "one of the basic civil rights of man. . . ."

Taken in its narrowest form, *Skinner* and its progeny stand for the proposition that married individuals have a fundamental right to coital procreation. A strong case can be made, however, to extend this right to unmarried persons. Indeed, in *Eisenstadt v. Baird*, the court stated that "[i]f the right of privacy means anything, it is the right of the *individual, married or single*, to be free from unwarranted governmental intrusion into matters so fundamentally affecting a person as the decision whether to bear or beget a child."

Moreover, because all cases decided by the court thus far have dealt with coital reproduction, it is unclear to what extent, if at all, noncoital forms of reproduction, such as artificial insemination, IVF [in vitro fertilization], or cloning, are constitutionally protected. The court's language regarding "procreation" and "bear[ing] or beget[ting] a child" is clearly broad enough to encompass noncoital forms of procreation. But since these issues were not before the court, it is not clear whether we should presume that the fundamental right of procreation is limited to sexual intercourse. Perhaps it means something slightly broader but still not so broad as to encompass cloning, such as any form of sexual procreation (which would include ARTs [assisted reproductive technologies] such as IVF or artificial insemination) but not asexual procreation.

Very little case law exists to help answer these questions because neither the states nor the federal government have prohibited the use of existing ARTs. Moreover, when the government has tried to differentiate between procreation by intercourse and procreation through the use of ARTs, the lower courts have generally upheld the right of individuals to use ARTs. . . .

In *Lindley v. Sullivan*, the plaintiffs adopted a son and soon thereafter applied for Child Insurance Benefits (CIB) that are generally provided to the disabled and other beneficiaries of the Social Security Act. The Social Security Administration denied the Lindleys' application for CIB, because the Social Security Act explicitly stated that CIB was not available to parents who adopted children after the beneficiary became entitled to Social Security benefits. In contrast, parents who conceived children through coitus or ARTs after the beneficiary became entitled to benefits *were* entitled to CIB. The Lindleys challenged the disparate treatment between adoptive parents and natural parents, asserting that such disparity violated the equal protection clause. The Lindleys asserted that the Seventh Circuit should apply strict scrutiny to the law in question, because the disparate treatment between adoptive and natural parents violated the fundamental right to procreation which, they further asserted, included the right to adopt children. The Seventh Circuit declined the Lindleys' invitation to proclaim that the fundamental right to procreation included a right of adoption, stating that there were "critical distinctions" between adoption and procreation. More importantly for purposes of this [viewpoint], however, in dicta [in their opinion] the Seventh Circuit cited *Griswold [v. Connecticut]* and stated that "the rights to marry and to procreate biologically are older than any state law and, for that matter, older than the Constitution or the Bill of Rights." Thus stated, the court suggested that while the fundamental right of procreation may not reach so far as to entitle an individual to adopt nonbiologically related children, it does protect an individual's right to "procreate biologically," which presumably would include the use of ARTs. The court in *Lindley* was not, of course, being asked to decide whether ARTs fall within the ambit of the right of procreation. But the court acknowledged that such a right existed and that it was fundamental. The court further suggested that a critical factor in determining the scope of this fundamental right is biological linkage between parent and child, a linkage that exists with intercourse and ARTs, but not adoption.

One additional case, *Lifchez v. Hartigan*, squarely presented this issue to a district court: whether the right of procreation included the right to use an ART, specifically, IVF. The court held that reproductive technology use is constitutionally protected, stating, "It takes no great leap of logic to see that within the cluster of constitutionally protected choices that includes the right to have access to contraceptives, there must be included within that cluster the right to submit to a medical procedure that may bring about, rather than prevent, pregnancy."

The *Lifchez* court's rationale is compelling. Individuals have a right under *Griswold v. Connecticut* to use contraceptives and a right under *Roe v. Wade* to abort a fetus, both of which indicate a broader right to prevent or terminate pregnancy. Moreover, under *Skinner* and *Eisenstadt*, individuals have a right to be free from forced sterilization, which indicates a broader right to bear or beget a child. These cases, viewed as a coherent whole, reveal that the constitutional right protected by the court thus far is not likely a narrow right to be free from forced sterilization, to obtain birth control, or to obtain an early-term abortion. Rather, the right is one of procreational autonomy, the fundamental right to decide whether, when, and how to bear or beget a child.

Because cloning is merely an asexual form of procreation, it is arguably as much a fundamental constitutional right as our right to procreate by either passion or the petri dish. . . .

Cloning Should Not Be Banned

If our Constitution does, in fact, give us the right to procreate by cloning, should we be afraid? Should we begin mobilizing politically in an attempt to pass a constitutional amendment via the procedures of Article V to ban human cloning? The answer should be "no," for several reasons.

First, the science fiction abuses associated with human cloning are unlikely to occur under current law, both statutory and constitutional. The current legal construct provides us with both the fundamental freedom to procreate as well as corresponding protections for the products of our procreation, our children, regardless of how they are conceived. Current law, in short, does not recognize genetic classification of human beings; if one is human, then one is entitled to all the legal rights enjoyed by other humans.

Second, the primary objections to human cloning appear to be unfounded, based more on morality, theology, and fear than objective data. Such subjective notions should not provide the sort of important or compelling interest sufficient to justify infringement of constitutional rights. Finally, even assuming that banning human cloning would serve one or more important or compelling governmental interests, such a law may nonetheless be unconstitutional because there are numerous, more narrowly tailored means—short of a total prohibition—by which to effectuate such ends.

Banning human cloning sends the regrettable message that politics and public pressure triumph over logic and the law. If citizens and lawmakers can just remember that clones are people, too, we can face this brave new world, confident that our laws are adequate to carry us all, safely, into the twenty-first century.

"*Rules must serve to prevent misuse, but they also should not unduly inhibit medical research that is guided by the ethical principle to help and cure existing human beings.*"

Research Cloning Should Be Allowed but Not Reproductive Cloning

Christiane Nüsslein-Volhard

In the following viewpoint, Christiane Nüsslein-Volhard argues that regulations are needed to govern medical technologies such as embryonic stem cell research, in vitro fertilization, and cloning. These regulations, contends Nüsslein-Volhard, should be based on reality, not fiction; they should be guided by science but decided on by society through its elected officials. Based on a biology-based definition of the beginning of a human being, regulations that prohibit reproductive cloning while allowing research cloning would be reasonable, asserts Nüsslein-Volhard. According to her, such regulations would prevent misuse but would not impede important medical research that can help existing human beings. Christiane Nüsslein-Volhard is a German biologist who won the Albert Lasker Basic Medical Research Award in 1991 and the Nobel Prize in physiology or medicine in 1995 for her research on the genetic control of embryonic development. She is the author of Coming to Life: How Genes Drive Development, *from which this viewpoint is excerpted.*

As you read, consider the following questions:

1. According to Nüsslein-Volhard, Paracelsus's recipe for the creation of the Homunculus calls for sperm to be incubated in a concoction of what?

2. According to Nüsslein-Volhard, what is the second reason that cloning does not work efficiently for the actual reproduction and breeding of animals?

3. In what important way do mammalian embryos differ from those of chickens or frogs, as stated by the author?

Genes and embryos have become the subject of intense public discussion, as the achievements and scientific discoveries in the fields of embryology and genetics not only increase our knowledge, but open up new possibilities to influence human life in a principally novel way. In addition, these achievements give rise to speculations and scenarios that indeed would change the world substantially should they ever be realized. Although several medical applications of new technologies, in particular gene technology, now are widely accepted, there is a widespread fear of the dangers of unpredictable consequences of such technologies.

Embryos Are at the Center of Debate

At the center of these debates is the issue of the extent to which human embryos should be manipulated in vitro and whether to interfere with their genetic constitution. Among different countries, the regulations relating to this issue are diverse, ranging from very restrictive, for instance in Germany and Ireland, to quite permissive in the United Kingdom and Sweden.

What exactly is the issue? Since 1978, it has been possible to fertilize human eggs outside the female body and cultivate the embryos in vitro for a short while before they are transferred back into the uterus to achieve pregnancy. The current procedure for this in vitro fertilization yields surplus embryos that are not transferred back. This opens up the possibility to use these embryos for medical research rather than discarding them. For instance, embryonic stem cell cultures could be obtained that could be used to develop therapies for several severe diseases. By genetic screening of such early embryos, congenital diseases could be avoided, even eradicated. However, according to the generally accepted moral conviction of our culture, every human being possesses dignity and, therefore, must not be used solely for the benefit of others. Opponents and supporters of embryo research share this moral position. The conflict therefore does not concern the acceptance of human dignity and protection, but rather the moral status of the early embryo.

From which point on is a human embryo a human being? Are the very early embryos human beings, which have to be protected just like growing embryos during pregnancy, or is their moral status different, and gradually changing until birth? The view of such a graded increase in status in many ways does reflect our natural feeling, which is manifested by our customs of birth control and laws of abortion. This difference in status is the bone of contention. The German law of 1990, for instance, defines the beginning of a human being at fertilization, while others consider the actual time of implantation into the female organism as crucial. In the U.K. [United Kingdom], in vitro is allowed until the 14th day. A human being becomes a legal person only by birth.

Although the criteria used for the definitions rely on biological events, they are not a scientific, but a moral, issue. Dignity, right to life, and protection are not biological, but moral categories. Therefore, these issues should be decided not by scientists but by our society as a whole through our political representatives. The big differences among nations even of very similar cultural backgrounds indicate that there is no single correct solution. However, in order to guarantee efficient research, we need clear regulations that are respected widely. The legal definition of the beginning of a human being should be reasonable, plausible, and consistent. It is at this point where scientific knowledge and judgment may help by describing grades and steps of embryonic development. It also is the obligation of scientists to reveal the potential applications and consequences of embryonic research. As there are conflicting moral issues—such as the right to life on the one hand and the pain and suffering caused by yet untreatable diseases on the other—these regulations demand great care and foresight and will have long-lasting consequences to our societies.

Utopias of Human Creation

Using early human embryos for medical therapy merely is part of the debate. Additional issues include the ability to interfere with the processes of reproduction, and diagnostic procedures such as the selection, or even the genetic manipulation, of children with desired attributes. A particularly controversial issue is that of cloning. It is remarkable that, in this debate, or rather in the representation of this debate by the media, there is little or no distinction between what is real, what is plausible, and what is utterly utopian. Sometimes the impression is conveyed that science not only could accomplish anything we desire, but actually would test the limits of the possible without any ethical considerations. This attitude is not new. There is a long tradition on both sides: blind belief in scientific progress and its flip side, the utter distrust in science.

Utopias of man creating man have existed since antiquity, handed down through the generations by way of myths and religions. Even though most people would acknowledge that the creation of woman from Adam's rib or the creation of Pallas Athena from Zeus's head are meant purely as symbols, things look different if such ideas are supported by contemporary biological theories. A good example from the Middle Ages is the recipe of the creation of the Homunculus (Latin for little human) by Paracelsus of Hohenheim, a scholar of alchemy and various other sciences in the 16th century. The story of the Homunculus is based on the popular idea of preformation, which prevailed for a long time. This idea implies that the sperm already harbors a completely formed human being, a Homunculus, which unfolds in the mother's body in the way a plant's seed would develop in the earth. Paracelsus's 1537 "recipe" replaces the mother's organism with an artificial medium. The sperm is incubated in a concoction of horse dung, urine, and other ingredients, and kept warm inside a pumpkin. According to Paracelsus, a small human being would appear within 40 days, provided that the process was undertaken in secrecy.

While the Homunculus story belongs to the realm of fantasy, British writer Aldous Huxley's utopia of human creation as described in his 1932 novel *Brave New World* often is considered to be rather realistic—at least if it is not possible right now, it is seen to be possible in the near future. Huxley imagines a procedure by which embryos can be made to form buds, such that from one embryo several identical copies can develop. These cloned embryos then are to be raised in bottles that serve as a kind of artificial uterus. The realism of his story is buttressed by Huxley's detailed description of the physical and technical difficulties of the uterus machine. Most

We Must Not Unwittingly Ban Research Cloning

Before we support a worldwide ban on cloning, we need to carefully examine the ethical language used and be sure it reflects the common good. By adopting vague ethical language we are making ourselves vulnerable to manipulation by those with a broader policy agenda than just banning reproductive cloning. We must watch carefully as human dignity is employed to ban human reproductive cloning, for it can unwittingly set the stage for banning other reproductive technologies such as IVF [in vitro fertilization], genetic testing and genetic modification, as well as therapeutic cloning [research cloning].

Kathryn Hinsch and Linda MacDonald Glenn,
"Worldwide Reproductive Cloning Bans:
The Danger of Misusing 'Human Dignity,'"
Women's Bioethics Project, May 2009.
www.womensbioethics.org.

striking perhaps is his conjecture that the conditions under which the clones mature can be manipulated to program the desired attributes of these parentless beings. In Huxley's time, the conditions of human and mammalian development were known in broad strokes only, and the nature and biochemical function of genes were not known at all. Yet, it is even more remarkable that there are people who take Huxley's ideas as present or future truth rather than as the fiction that they are.

Research from Animals to Humans

While our understanding of the general processes involved in human development has been aided by research on model organisms, such as the mouse, procedures discussed for application in humans are based on research on domestic animals.

Artificial fertilization as well as genetic diagnosis of single embryonic cells have been developed and studied in cattle. The
original idea was to use genetic diagnosis to predetermine the
sex of a calf in order to produce predominantly female cattle
for milk or male cattle for meat, depending on the breed. The
procedure rarely is used, though, because it is so complicated.

For artificial fertilization, hormone treatment of the cow
stimulates the production of supernumerary [i.e., extra] eggs.
Then the eggs are removed from the ovary and placed in a
culture dish where they are mixed either with the sperm, or
where the sperm is injected directly into the eggs. After a few
days, when the fertilized egg has divided several times, the
embryo is reimplanted into the mother cow. For genetic diagnosis, prior to implantation, one or two cells are removed
from the embryo and its chromosomes are analyzed. The removal of one or even two cells at this stage does not harm the
embryo, and it will develop normally after implantation.

The first experiments in cloning by nuclear transplantation were conducted in the 1960s on amphibia. Researchers
were interested in determining whether all body cells maintain
all genes that are necessary to create a healthy animal. The
first mammal to be cloned was a sheep called Dolly. Breeders'
interest in cloning lies in multiplying genetically identical animals that have proven to have particular desired properties.
This also is the basis for the wide use of cloning in crops.
However, plants are not cloned by cell nucleus transfer but
rather by taking layers and cuttings for plant reproduction, a
quite natural event propagating genetically identical plants.

During the procedure of animal cloning, the nucleus of an
egg cell is removed and replaced by a nucleus taken from a
body cell of a chosen animal. In rare cases, a blastocyst will
develop and, even rarer still, this blastocyst will give rise to a
healthy animal. Such a cloned animal carries the same genotype as the donor animal from which the nucleus originated.
Even though cloning has been accomplished in several ani-

mals—among them cows, sheep, and mice—the success rate is extremely low. In most cases, the clone's development is sooner or later interrupted, resulting in frequent miscarriages and stillbirths.

While these attempts at cloning animals have provided a satisfactory answer to the question of whether the set of genes remains complete in body cells, cloning does not work efficiently for the actual reproduction and breeding of animals. There are several reasons for this. First, the body cells from which the nuclei are taken may have accumulated too many mutations. During normal development, special cells from the germ line produce the offspring. These cells are well protected, leading to fewer mutations than body cells. Second, the developmental potential of body cells is restricted because their genes are wrapped in special proteins and partially modified. These restrictions would have to be reversed completely during contact with the cytoplasm of the egg. This reprogramming apparently takes place only rarely. A probable third reason is that, in the egg, the chromosomes are not always distributed in an orderly fashion after the nuclear transfer. Whatever the reasons may be, the fact is that cloning by nuclear transfer is successful only in very rare cases. Presently, it is unpredictable how the procedure could be made more efficient and safe.

Human Reproductive Cloning Has Been Roundly Rejected

Cloning a human means creating a person with exactly the same genotype as an already existing person—a belated twin, as it were. To construct such an embryo, the nucleus of a body cell would have to be transferred to an egg cell from which its own nucleus had been removed. Yet, as previously stated, cloning animals with this procedure only rarely produces healthy animals. In Dolly's case, more than 200 eggs had to be treated before success was achieved. This rate is much too low to justify even the slightest attempt at cloning a human being. With humans, vastly different safety requirements are appropriate than those for domestic animals. While it is a moot point to debate the ethical implications of a procedure that, although theoretically possible, in reality cannot be performed successfully—at least not for the time being—human imagination still has stirred up extensive ethical discussions on the issue of cloning. Biologically speaking—apart from the extremely low success rate and frequent mishaps predicted to go with this procedure—the fact that a cloned child would have no parents creates a high level of discomfort. In addition, the motivation for a desire to "double" oneself or somebody else does not bode well for the child's welfare. Therefore, on ethical grounds alone, attempts at cloning of human beings (reproductive cloning) have been rejected by scientists and researchers all over the world. In many countries it even has been rendered illegal. . . .

When the Embryo Requires Protection

Still, the crucial issue remains: When does a human embryo have to be protected against destruction and use for other purposes? As mentioned, it is not the task of the scientists to decide this question, but rather that of society as a whole, and the differences in political opinions reflect by no means a discrepancy of the opinions of scientists in different countries.

Nevertheless, in defining the moral status of the embryo, the classical arguments of ethicists and philosophers often are based on pieces of biological evidence, which sometimes prove to be highly debatable if inspected more closely from the view of modern biology. For instance, a widely accepted dogma argues that human life is a continuous process, starting with fertilization, which does not display any sharp transitions—and during which nothing substantial is being added that would justify a change in status. Another argument states that the zygote—with its complete genetic constitution—also would hold the complete potential to develop into a human being.

Now, it is quite clear that a chicken or frog embryo starting with fertilization has the potential, even without motherly protection, to develop continuously until hatching. In the case of mammals—and thus humans—however, the embryo has to implant into the uterus of the mother to be able to develop further. The zygote alone only has the potential to form a blastocyst that then has to hatch from the egg case in order to implant into the uterus and begin the next stage of development.

Biologically speaking, this is a marked transition and there almost is nothing more discontinuous than such a process in which the embryo is placing itself in direct and immediate cellular contact with another individual. In the fertilized egg, the genetic program is complete. For its realization, though, the intensive interaction—the symbiosis with a second organism, the mother—is required. This is indispensable and cannot be provided by surrogates. Only at birth, the growing human being has become a separated, independent organism that breathes with its own independent metabolism. Certainly, the born human being still has much need of attention and protection, but it now is fed from the outside and, therefore, in case of necessity, can survive without the mother. There is no debate that, at this stage, it is a human being with all rights.

Rules That Do Not Impede Medical Research Are Needed

As already mentioned, it is remarkable that the issue of embryo protection is treated in such a different manner in different countries. This reflects the difficulty in compromising between extreme positions. It would be most desirable if one could agree on rules guiding embryonic research that are based on plausible and reasonable grounds. Science is international and progress in the long run depends on equal and just conditions for scientific research. Such rules certainly must serve to prevent misuse, but they also should not unduly inhibit medical research that is guided by the ethical principle to help and cure existing human beings.

In addition to the scientific quality of the intended research, it should be required that sufficient animal experiments have been carried out in order to guarantee a reasonable rate of success to make a procedure practicable in humans. Also, the laws should prevent those embryos manipulated in vitro—for example chimeras with embryonic stem cells, or those that have been constructed by nuclear transfer—from being implanted into a female organism to start pregnancy. Such a regulation also would prohibit reproductive cloning of humans. The most important factor, however, is to proceed with care and ensure that possible contributions of medical research to reduce pain and suffering are not prohibited for fear of misuse.

> *"If we are to realize the full therapeutic and scientific potential of human embryonic stem cell research, stem cell lines derived by [somatic cell nuclear transfer] and other methods must be eligible for federal funding."*

Research Cloning Should Receive Federal Funding

Association of American Universities

In the following viewpoint, the Association of American Universities (AAU) contends that embryonic stem cells derived from somatic cell nuclear transfer (SCNT), i.e, from research cloning, should be eligible for federal funding. The AAU says that research cloning is necessary to obtain stem cells that are genetically matched to patients, and therefore, will not elicit an immune response. According to the AAU, research cloning is necessary to derive the full benefits of human embryonic stem cell research. Prohibiting federal funding for this kind of research is not ethically or legally justified, says the AAU. The Association of American Universities is an organization of sixty-one universities in the United States, including Harvard, Princeton, the University of California, and the University of Michigan.

As you read, consider the following questions:

1. The AAU joins with patient advocacy and scientific communities in expressing disappointment that stem cells derived from what procedures are excluded from NIH funding?

2. According to AAU, the greatest scientific opportunity arises from the ability of scientists to work with stem cell lines that can model what?

3. The AAU states that it understands that NIH-funded scientists must adhere to the legal limitations imposed by what amendment? What does this amendment prohibit?

The President's [Barack Obama's] executive order of March 9, 2009, which lifted the constraints on NIH [National Institutes of Health] funding for human stem cell research (hESC) established in 2001, was an inspirational moment for the biomedical research enterprise, the scientists who will pursue this promising research and, most importantly, for the patients and their families who will see its therapeutic benefits. We commend NIH for its swift issuance of draft guidelines to implement the executive order. Our faculty and institutions are anxious to begin new hESC research and the President's executive order and NIH's prompt action will enable them to pursue scientific advances this year [2009].

Although we are supportive of the executive order and NIH's proposed guidelines, and look forward to working with the administration in implementing them, we do have . . . concerns with what has been proposed. . . .

The limitation of federally funded research to hESCs derived from surplus in vitro fertilization (IVF) embryos is unnecessarily narrow, and is neither scientifically, ethically nor legally justified. AAU [Association of American Universities] joins with the patient advocacy and scientific communities in expressing disappointment that hESC lines derived from somatic cell nuclear transfer (SCNT), parthenogenesis and IVF embryos created for research purposes are excluded from NIH-funded research.

To be sure, there is great scientific and therapeutic promise in hESC research using stem cell lines derived from surplus IVF embryos. The scientific opportunities in developmental biology; new understandings of the interplay of genetics and the environment in human development and disease genesis and progression; and, ultimately, the possibility that hESC research will lead to therapies in which diseased organs and tissues can be targeted or replaced by tissues derived from stem cells have made this research among the most exciting and promising lines of scientific inquiry at the dawn of this new century.

The Importance of Genetically Matched Stem Cells

However, the shortest path to all of the promise of stem cell research is through stem cell lines derived by SCNT from living patients. Such tissues will be an exact genetic match for the patient and therefore, prevent immune rejection of transplanted tissue or the need for immunosuppressive drugs that cause further stress to patients and leave them vulnerable to other infections and side effects. As the National Academies explains in the 2001 report, "Stem Cells and the Future of Regenerative Medicine":

> A substantial obstacle to the success of transplantation of any cells, including stem cells and their derivatives, is the immune-mediated rejection of foreign tissue by the recipient's body. In current stem cell transplantation procedures with bone marrow and blood, success can hinge on obtaining a close match between donor and recipient tissues and on the use of immunosuppressive drugs, which often have severe and life-threatening side effects. To ensure that

The Public Supports Research Cloning

US federal government policy largely conforms to public opinion, but with a striking exception. Funding for research on therapeutic cloning has long been banned. Nonetheless, public opinion strongly supports it. In a democratic society, deferring to objections from a small (mainly religious) minority and limiting research that has so much therapeutic promise may well be unethical.

M.D.R. Evans and Jonathan Kelley,
"US Attitudes Toward Human Embryonic Stem Cell Research,"
Nature Biotechnology, *June 2011.*

stem cell–based therapies can be broadly applicable for many conditions and individuals, new means to overcome the problem of tissue rejection must be found. Although ethically controversial, somatic cell nuclear transfer, a technique that produces a lineage of stem cells that are genetically identical to the donor, promises such an advantage. Other options for this purpose include genetic manipulation of the stem cells and the development of a very large bank of embryonic stem cell lines. In conjunction with research on stem cell biology and the development of stem cell therapies, research on approaches that prevent immune rejection of stem cells and stem cell–derived tissues should be actively pursued.

Nuclear Transplantation Provides the Greatest Promise

However promising stem cell lines from surplus IVF embryos may be, the scientific and therapeutic promise of cell lines from SCNT, parthenogenesis and IVF embryos created for research purposes is far greater. NIH and federally supported scientists must be able to work with stem cell lines that have been derived from sources other than IVF embryos, lines in which the genomes of such cell lines can be selected or, as appropriate and ethical, designed. The greatest scientific opportunity arises from the ability of scientists to work with stem cell lines that can model the earliest stages of human development and disease development and progression. As was explained in the 2002 National Academies report "Scientific and Medical Aspects of Human Reproductive Cloning":

> In addition to possible uses in therapeutic transplantation, embryonic stem cells and cell lines derived by nuclear transplantation could be valuable tools for both fundamental and applied medical and biological research. This research would begin with the transfer of genetically defined donor nuclei from normal and diseased tissues. The resulting cell lines could be used to study how inherited and acquired alterations of genetic components might contribute to disease processes. The properties of the cell lines could be studied directly, or the embryonic stem cells could be studied as they differentiate into other cell types. For example, the way in which cells derived by nuclear transplantation from an Alzheimer's disease patient acted while differentiating into brain cells, compared with those derived from a normal patient, might yield new clues about Alzheimer's disease. Such cell lines could also be used to ensure that research covers a more genetically diverse human population than that represented in the blastocysts stored in IVF clinics, promoting studies of the causes and consequences of genetic diseases by allowing researchers to study how embryonic stem cells with different genetic endowments differ in the way that they form cell types and tissues. Finally, studies of genetic reprogramming and genetic imprinting will be substantially enhanced through the use of stem cells derived by nuclear transplantation, compared with studies with stem cells derived from other sources.

AAU's member presidents and chancellors have long been committed to the derivation of stem cells through SCNT, as the AAU Statement on Human Cloning, adopted by the AAU membership on April 23, 2002, attests:

> AAU therefore supports nuclear transplantation to produce stem cells, also known as somatic cell nuclear transfer, as nonreproductive cloning, and as therapeutic cloning. AAU concurs with the NAS [National Academy of Sciences] that nuclear transplantation to produce stem cells has considerable potential for advancing our fundamental knowledge and developing new medical therapies to treat debilitating diseases. Continuing the investigation of stem cells produced by nuclear transplantation is the only way to assure that the value of this nascent technology is realized. Before applications to humans should be considered, we need further study of cells derived from the process of nuclear transplantation, subject to federal safeguards.

AAU understands that NIH-funded scientists must adhere to the legal limitations imposed by the Dickey-Wicker Amendment, prohibiting federal funding for any research in which a human embryo is created or destroyed for such research. But, the draft guidelines put the situation best: "Although human embryonic stem cells are derived from embryos, such stem cells are not themselves human embryos."

Although SCNT is only a theoretical possibility at this point, the technical barriers to its successful use are falling away rapidly, and it will likely become widely available—and used in the private sector and in privately supported research—in coming months or years. Furthermore, as SCNT is one of only three methods of deriving stem cells, along with derivation from IVF embryos and derivation using iPSC [induced pluripotent stem cells], it would be unwise to exclude this method from those available to the scientific community for research of benefit to human health. This work can be done in full compliance with ethical and legal considerations.

If we are to realize the full therapeutic and scientific potential of human embryonic stem cell research, cell lines derived by SCNT and other methods must be eligible for federal funding.

> "The composition of food products from cattle, swine, and goat clones, or the offspring of any animal clones, is no different from that of conventionally bred animals."

Cloned Meat Is Safe and Does Not Need to Be Labeled

US Food and Drug Administration

In the following viewpoint, the US Food and Drug Administration (FDA) asserts that food from cloned cattle, goats, and pigs is no different than food from non-cloned, or conventional animals; therefore, there is no reason to label meat from cloned animals. The FDA says it has been studying the safety of cloned meat for at least five years and has not found any increased human health risks. Cloned meat from cattle, goats, and pigs is safe, says the government agency. The Food and Drug Administration is an agency of the US Department of Health and Human Services and is responsible for regulating food safety.

US Food and Drug Administration, "Animal Cloning and Food Safety," US Food and Drug Administration, January 2008.

As you read, consider the following questions:

1. When it became apparent in 2001 that cloning could be a commercial venture to help improve the quality of herds, the FDA asked livestock producers to voluntarily do what?

2. According to the FDA, its concern about animal health prompted it to do what?

3. According to the FDA, clones may allow farmers to provide more copies of their best animals, those with naturally occurring traits such as what?

After years of detailed study and analysis, the Food and Drug Administration [FDA] has concluded that meat and milk from clones of cattle, swine (pigs), and goats, and the offspring of clones from any species traditionally consumed as food, are as safe to eat as food from conventionally bred animals. This conclusion stems from an extensive study of animal cloning and related food safety, culminating in the release of three FDA documents in January 2008: a risk assessment, a risk management plan, and guidance for industry.

Researchers have been cloning livestock species since 1996, starting with the famous sheep named Dolly. When it became apparent in 2001 that cloning could become a commercial venture to help improve the quality of herds, FDA's Center for Veterinary Medicine (CVM) asked livestock producers to voluntarily keep food from clones and their offspring out of the food chain until CVM could further evaluate the issue.

FDA Studies Cloning

For more than five years, CVM scientists studied hundreds of published reports and other detailed information on clones of livestock animals to evaluate the safety of food from these animals. The resulting report, called a risk assessment, presents FDA's conclusions that

- cloning poses no unique risks to animal health, compared to the risks found with other reproduction methods, including natural mating

- the composition of food products from cattle, swine, and goat clones, or the offspring of any animal clones, is no different from that of conventionally bred animals

- because of the preceding two conclusions, there are no additional risks to people eating food from cattle, swine, and goat clones or the offspring of any animal clones traditionally consumed as food

FDA issued the risk assessment, the risk management plan, and guidance for industry in draft form for public comment in December 2006. Since that time, FDA has updated the risk assessment to reflect new scientific information that reinforces the food safety conclusions of the draft.

"Our additional review only serves to strengthen our conclusions on food safety," says Stephen F. Sundlof, D.V.M., Ph.D., director of FDA's Center for Food Safety and Applied Nutrition. "Meat and milk from cow, pig, and goat clones, and the offspring of any animal clones, are as safe as food we eat every day."

FDA's concern about animal health prompted the agency to develop a risk management plan to decrease any risks to animals involved in cloning. FDA also issued guidance to clone producers and the livestock industry on using clones and their offspring for human food and animal feed.

What Is a Clone?

"Clones are genetic copies of an animal," says Larisa Rudenko, Ph.D., a molecular biologist and senior adviser for biotechnology in CVM. "They're similar to identical twins, but born at different times." Cloning can be thought of as an extension of the assisted reproductive technologies that livestock breeders

United Kingdom Food Standards Agency: Cloned Food Is Safe

The FSA [United Kingdom Food Standards Agency] Board met today [December 7, 2010] and discussed animal cloning for food production, including recent developments on this issue, following the board's initial discussion in September.

The board agreed to advise ministers that:

- the marketing of products obtained from cloned animals should be subject to authorisation as novel foods

- based on the current evidence, there are no food safety grounds for regulating foods from the descendants of cloned cattle and pigs

- the FSA is minded to adopt the position taken by the European Commission and others, that food obtained from the descendants of clones of cattle and pigs does not require authorisation under the novel foods regulation

- the board will seek the views of interested parties in relation to this change of position, and will return to this matter in the future if new information makes this necessary

In respect of other consumer interests, the board:

- agreed that, for food safety purposes, mandatory labelling of meat and milk obtained from the descendants of cloned cattle and pigs would be unnecessary and disproportionate, providing no significant food safety benefit to consumers

Food Standards Agency, "Meat and Milk from Cloned Animals," December 7, 2010. www.food.gov.uk.

have been using for centuries, such as artificial insemination, and more recently, embryo transfer and in vitro fertilization.

Animal cloning has been around for more than 20 years. Most cloning today uses a process called somatic cell nuclear transfer:

- Scientists take an egg from a female animal (often from ovaries at the slaughterhouse) and remove the gene-containing nucleus.

- The nucleus of a cell from an animal the breeder wishes to copy is added to the egg.

- After other steps in the laboratory take place, the egg cell begins to form into an embryo.

- The embryo is implanted in the uterus of a surrogate dam (female parent), which carries it to term and delivers it like her own offspring.

Clones may allow farmers to upgrade the quality of their herds by providing more copies of their best animals—those with naturally occurring desirable traits, such as resistance to disease, high milk production, or quality meat production. These animal clones are then used for conventional breeding, and their sexually reproduced offspring become the food-producing animals.

What Cloning Means to Consumers

- FDA has concluded that cattle, swine, and goat clones, and the offspring of any animal clones traditionally consumed as food, are safe for human and animal consumption.

- Food labels do not have to state that food is from animal clones or their offspring. FDA has found no science-based reason to require labels to distinguish between products from clones and products from conventionally produced animals.

- The main use of clones is to produce breeding stock, not food. These animal clones—copies of the best animals in the herd—are then used for conventional breeding, and the sexually reproduced offspring of the animal clones become the food-producing animals.

- Due to the lack of information on clone species other than cow, goat, and pig (for example, sheep), FDA recommends that other clone species do not enter the human food supply.

> "According to the three standards used to determine if cloned food is safe—nutrition, toxicology, and chemical compositions—eating cancerous tissue or pus would also be safe."

The Safety of Cloned Meat Is Uncertain and It Should Be Labeled

Martha Rosenberg

In the following viewpoint, Martha Rosenberg maintains that Americans could unwittingly be eating potentially unsafe cloned meat. Rosenberg says that the veracity of the US Food and Drug Administration's report declaring cloned meat safe is questionable. She says the report raises many questions about the health of cloned animals and the safety of their meat and milk. According to Rosenberg, cloned food should be labeled so American consumers can decide for themselves whether they want to eat cloned food. Martha Rosenberg is a writer who focuses on the pharmaceutical and food industries. Her work has appeared in the Boston Globe, San Francisco Chronicle, *and* Chicago Tribune. *She plans to publish a book, entitled* Born with a Junk Food Deficiency: How Flaks, Quacks and Hacks Pimp the Public Health.

As you read, consider the following questions:

1. What is the name of the "reprogramming problem," according to Rosenberg?

2. According to Rosenberg, what did the FDA report say about rats fed cloned meat and milk who exhibited greater "frequency of vocalization"?

3. According to Rosenberg, what did the World Society for the Protection of Animals observe about animal suffering in the cloning process?

It's just a matter of time before we are eating clones, if we are not eating them now.

When Canadian agricultural leaders asked Agriculture Secretary Tom Vilsack last week [August 2010] after a scandal about unlabeled clone products in Europe if "cloned cows or their offspring have made it into the North American food supply," he said, "I can't say today that I can answer your question in an affirmative or negative way. I don't know."

And when AlterNet asked the USDA [United States Department of Agriculture] this week if cloned products are already in the food supply, a spokesman said the department was "not aware of an instance where product from an animal clone has entered the food supply" thanks to a "voluntary moratorium"—but that offspring of clones, at the heart of the Europe scandal, "are not clones and are therefore not included" in the voluntary moratorium.

Sounds like Europe is not the only place eating milk and meat from unlabeled clone offspring. In fact, the BBC, UK newspapers and even a US grocer all report that US consumers are digging into clone food, whether or not they know it.

The FDA Report Is Not Convincing

Like bovine growth hormone and Roundup Ready crops, the government says clone products are so safe they don't need to be labeled. But the 2008 FDA [Food and Drug Administration] report, "Animal Cloning: A Risk Assessment" and a report from the European Food Safety Authority released at the same time, raise questions about the health of cloned animals, the safety of their milk and meat and even the soundness of the clone process itself.

To clone an animal, "scientists start with a piece of ear skin and mince it up in a lab. Then they induce the cells to divide in a culture dish until they forget they are skin cells and regain their ability to express all of their genes," writes the *Los Angeles Times*' Karen Kaplan. "Meanwhile, the nucleus is removed from a donor egg and placed next to a skin cell. Both are zapped with a tiny electric shock, and if all goes well the egg grows into a genetic copy of the original animal."

So far so good except that it turns out many clones lack the ability to "reprogram the somatic nucleus of the donor to the state of a fertilized zygote," says the FDA report and be the perfect replica a clone is supposed to be.

The reprogamming problem, called epigenetic dysregulation, means many clones—some say 90 percent—are born with deformities, enlarged umbilical cords, respiratory distress, heart and intestine problems and large offspring syndrome, the latter often killing the clone and its "mother," the surrogate dam. Clones that survive epigenetic dysregulation often require surgery, oxygen and transfusions at birth, eat insatiably but do not necessarily gain weight and fail to maintain normal temperatures, admits the report.

While denying that such dysregulation is endemic to cloning, the FDA report nonetheless reassures readers that "residual epigenetic reprogramming errors that could persist" in clones will "reset" over time. The errors will also "reset" in off-

spring who, though "the same as any other sexually reproduced animals," may nonetheless have them. Oops.

The FDA report, written in collaboration with Elizabeth-
town, PA-based Cyagra and Austin, TX-based ViaGen, another
clone company, tries hard to talk around these and other
clone problems. Too hard.

Although clones' calcium, phosphorus, alkaline phos-
phatase and glucose levels exceed those seen in normal animals, "all of the elevations can be explained by the clones'
stage of life or stress level, and the increased levels observed
do not represent a food consumption risk," says the report.

The "slight mammary development" in a 4 1/2 month old
Jersey calf? Such precociousness "sometimes occurs in conventional heifers if they are overfed."

The rats fed cloned meat and milk who exhibited greater
"frequency of vocalization," a signal of emotional response? It
was probably "incidental and unrelated to treatment," says the
report.

Cloned meat samples that show "altered" fatty acid composition and delta-9 desaturase? "No comparisons were made
with historical reference values for either milk or meat," says
the report. Maybe it's an overall trend in meat and milk. . . .

Worse, the report relies on government regulation as usual
to catch clone aberrations in the food supply. Nutrition labeling requirements will determine if clone milk is okay says the
report since "determining whether animal clones are producing a hazardous substance in their milk although theoretically
possible, is highly impractical." (We can inject a nucleus into
an egg but can't analyze milk?)

And the hapless and sick throwaways that are cloning's by-
catch? Those animals won't be a threat to the food supply says
the FDA report, because they die at birth. And if they don't
die but remain sickly, they'll be kept out of the food supply by
the same slaughterhouse inspectors who kept out mad cows
. . . and *E. coli*. Bon appetit.

Cloned Meat Is Not Ready for Prime Time

FDA [US Food and Drug Administration] should institute a mandatory moratorium on food or feed from cloned animals until:

- The agency has established a mandatory pre-market review process, regulating cloning as a new animal drug and requiring generational studies including investigations into potential food safety threats from unexpected metabolites potentially created by the cloning process;

- The troubling animal cruelty issues from cloning are resolved and cloning can meet the highest standards for animal welfare;

- Full "environmental impact statements" show no harmful environmental impacts from the use of cloning; and

- An advisory committee has addressed the many ethical issues around animal cloning, and broad public discussions have resolved the unique ethical and moral concerns raised by the technology.

Finally, if food from clones is deemed suitable for sale following the steps described above, FDA must require labeling of cloned food, to monitor for harmful effects (as advised by the NAS [National Academy of Sciences]) and to protect consumers who wish to avoid cloned food.

Center for Food Safety,
"Not Ready for Prime Time: FDA's Flawed Approach to
Assessing the Safety of Food from Animal Clones,"
March 2007. www.centerforfoodsafety.org.

"According to the three standards used to determine if cloned food is safe—nutrition, toxicology and chemical composition—eating cancerous tissue or pus would also be safe," Dr. Shiv Chopra, a veterinarian, microbiologist and human rights activist, told AlterNet when we asked about cloned food safety. It is like the wide-scale and unlabeled bovine growth hormone used to produce milk "in which a cow gene was inserted into *E. coli*," says Dr. Chopra—a huge experiment conducted on the public.

Even meat and restaurant interests agree with Dr. Chopra in written comments about cloning on the European Food Safety Authority (EFSA) website.

Despite the science, there is an "important limitation" to cloning projections says Coldiretti, Italy's largest farming interest group: "The impossibility to make prediction (sic) on a long-term base. The 'Inquiry into BSE' [mad cow] shows how no scientists had been able to foresee the problems connected to the practice of recycling animal proteins in herbivores feeding. The BSE prion needed around 50 years to develop."

CLITRAVI, the Brussels-based [Liaison Centre] for the Meat Processing Industry [in the European Union], concurs. "In the light of EFSA's own clearly expressed concerns regarding animal health and animal welfare, we take the view that further research is needed before offsprings of cloned animals are used for any purpose whatsoever, including medical," it wrote.

Consumers Should Have a Choice

The US-based Union of Concerned Scientists agrees that more research about cloning is necessary—not to mention labeling. "The choice of whether to purchase such foods should be in the hands of individual consumers, not the government or the industry. Consumers will have such a choice only if the foods are labeled," says the 250,000-member nonprofit science group.

In defending cloning, the FDA, Big Meat and Biotech claim its negatives are no worse than in vitro fertilization and other assisted reproductive technology (ART) techniques already entrenched in factory farms, and that it will aid "world hunger." Animal suffering is downplayed by simply not counting the animals who don't make it in final figures leading the World Society for the Protection of Animals to observe that welfare and mortality are not just risks for surviving clones but effects that "occur in a large proportion of surrogate dams and clones."

While the FDA admits that clone calves that "die or are euthanized due to poor health" are rendered into animal feed by-products that present "possible risks" to animals and the people who eat them, it is less worried about healthy clones. Healthies are "unlikely" to be used for human food "given their potential value as breeding stock" or even used as animal food, "except through rendering of dead clones that occurred at parturition or by accident."

Since the first cloned mammal, Dolly the sheep, was created in 1996, cloning has become more common and causes less outrage than new Frankenfoods like the Enviropig with its roundworm gene and AquAdvantage salmon with its Chinook salmon gene (both moving toward FDA approval.) But whether it's become common in our food no one can know—because it's unlabeled. And could be anywhere.

Periodical and Internet Sources Bibliography

The following articles have been selected to supplement the diverse views presented in this chapter.

Lorna Benson	"Bill Banning Human Cloning Rankles Researchers, Bio-Business Leaders," Minnesota Public Radio, March 17, 2011.
Economist	"The Status of the Unborn: A Person Already," October 8, 2011.
Pamela Foohey	"Paying Women for Their Eggs for Use in Stem Cell Research," *Pace Law Review*, Spring 2010.
Insoo Hyun and Paul Tesar	"Stem Cell: Cloning Advance Calls for Careful Regulation," *Nature*, October 6, 2011.
Leon R. Kass	"Defending Life and Dignity; How, Finally, to Ban Human Cloning," *Weekly Standard*, February 25, 2008.
Yuval Levin	"The Real Lessons of Stem Cells," *Newsweek*, March 30, 2009.
Loane Skene	"Recent Developments in Stem Cell Research: Social, Ethical, and Legal Issues for the Future," *Indiana Journal of Global Legal Studies*, Summer 2010.
Wesley J. Smith	"Federal Funding for Human Cloning?," *National Review Online*, September 23, 2010. www.nationalreview.com.
Bonnie Stabile	"Demographic Profile of States with Human Cloning Laws," *Politics and the Life Sciences*, March 2007.
Robert Streiffer	"Chimeras, Moral Status, and Public Policy," *Journal of Law, Medicine & Ethics*, Summer 2010.

Glossary

adult stem cells Multipotent stem cells derived from adult tissues that generally only give rise to the different specialized cell types of the tissue from which they originated.

assisted reproductive technology (ART) Fertility treatments that involve a laboratory handling eggs or embryos, such as in vitro fertilization.

blastocyst A very early embryonic stage of development (about three to six days old) consisting of approximately 150–300 cells and composed of an outer layer and an inner cell mass.

clone A genetically identical cell, tissue, individual, etc.

differentiation The process by which early unspecified cells become specialized cells such as heart, liver, muscle, or brain tissue.

DNA Deoxyribonucleic acid, the genetic material found primarily in the nucleus of cells that contains the instructions for making an individual organism.

embryo In humans, the developing organism from the moment of conception or fertilization through the eighth week of development.

embryonic stem cells Pluripotent stem cells derived from the inner cell mass of an embryo at the blastocyst stage that can generally give rise to any type of cell in the body except germ cells.

enucleated Having had its nucleus removed.

epigenetic Heritable changes in phenotype (appearance) or gene expression caused by mechanisms other than changes in the underlying DNA sequence.

fertilized egg cell An egg cell (oocyte) that has a full complement of genetic material and is capable of developing into a human being.

fetus In humans, the developing organism from the eighth week of development until birth.

gametes Mature haploid reproductive cells, such as an oocyte or a sperm cell, that can unite with another of the opposite sex and form a zygote.

genetic engineering A set of procedures whereby a specific piece of DNA can be excised from a chromosome and inserted into the DNA of a chromosome of a different organism.

germ cells Cells that give rise to either sperm or oocytes.

haploid A cell that contains one complete set of chromosomes, or half of the number in a mature organism.

in vitro Experiments that are performed outside an organism's body, in a test tube or a Petri dish.

in vitro fertilization (IVF) A procedure, commonly performed to help couples conceive, where an egg cell (oocyte) and a sperm cell are brought together in a Petri dish in the laboratory, to produce a fertilized egg that can be implanted in a woman's uterus and give rise to pregnancy.

in vivo Experiments that are performed within an organism's body.

induced pluripotent stem cell (iPSC) A type of pluripotent stem cell artificially derived from a non-pluripotent cell, typically an adult somatic cell, by inducing a "forced" expression of specific genes.

meiosis The type of cell division a diploid germ cell undergoes to produce gametes (sperm or eggs) that will carry half the normal chromosome number.

mitosis The type of cell division that allows a population of cells to increase its numbers or to maintain its numbers.

multipotent stem cells Stem cells that can give rise to a number of different specialized cell types, but all within a particular tissue. For example, blood-forming (hematopoietic) stem cells are multipotent cells that can produce all cell types that are normal components of the blood.

nucleus A part of the cell that is surrounded by a membrane and contains the DNA, or genetic instructions of the cell.

oocyte Female egg cell that normally provides half of the DNA to produce a human being.

parthenogenesis The artificial activation of an egg in the absence of a sperm; the egg begins to divide as if it has been fertilized.

pluripotent stem cells Stem cells that can generally specialize into any one of the over two hundred different types of cells found in the human body, except germ cells.

reproductive cloning Using the somatic cell nuclear transfer (SCNT) procedure for the purpose of creating a living human being that is a clone of the donor of the somatic cell used in the SCNT procedure.

somatic cell An adult cell; a cell from a fully developed organism; any adult bodily cell such as heart, skin, or muscle that typically has a full complement of DNA.

somatic cell nuclear transfer (SCNT) A process by which a nucleus from a somatic cell is transferred into an unfertilized egg (oocyte), from which the nucleus has been removed and the egg (that now has a full complement of DNA) is stimulated to begin development.

stem cell line Embryonic stem cells all of which are derived from a single embryo and are therefore genetically identical, which can be maintained and grown in Petri dishes for an infinite length of time.

sperm cell Male germ cell that generally provides half of the genetic material to produce a human being.

therapeutic cloning Using the somatic cell nuclear transfer (SCNT) procedure to produce an embryo for the purpose of extracting its stem cells and using them to replace damaged tissues in a patient. The SCNT created embryonic stem cells will be genetically identical to the donor of the somatic cell used in the SCNT procedure and thus they will not be rejected by the patient's immune system.

totipotent The ability of a cell to give rise to all the specialized cell types of an organism. Plant cells are generally totipotent.

zygote The earliest moment of human development; when the embryo consists of a single fertilized egg cell.

For Further Discussion

Chapter 1

1. Dan W. Brock contends that using somatic cell nuclear transfer to create an embryo for stem cell research is moral. However, William Saunders, Michael Fragoso, and David Prentice contend that it is not moral. Compare and contrast the main argument used to support each viewpoint. Which viewpoint do you agree with and why?

2. Right to Life of Michigan Education Fund opposes embryonic stem cell research and cloning, but thinks induced pluripotent stem cell (iPSC) research is ethical. Gregory E. Kaebnick says those who oppose embryonic stem cell research and cloning should also oppose iPSC research. Do you think Kaebnick's reasoning is correct? That is, do you think it is morally inconsistent to oppose embryonic stem cell research and cloning, but to promote iPSC research? Support your conclusion.

3. Bonnie Steinbock believes women who donate their eggs for research should be paid just like women who donate for reproductive purposes. Thomas Berg believes women who donate for research should not be paid. What do you think is Berg's opinion on paying women who donate their eggs for reproductive purposes? Support your answer.

Chapter 2

1. Gregg Easterbrook says human reproductive cloning is "natural," while Dennis P. Hollinger contends that cloning is unethical. Do you think when Easterbrook says cloning is natural he means it is ethical, and do you think when Hollinger says cloning is unethical he means unnatural?

Explain the connection between what humans think of as "natural" and what we think of as "ethical" in the context of human reproductive cloning.

2. Both Carson Strong and Joyce C. Havstad agree that parents have a right to reproductive freedom. On what specifically do they disagree? Explain using examples from the text.

Chapter 3

1. The Biotechnology Industry Organization contends that farm animal cloning is relatively safe, while the Humane Society of the United States contends that it is not. Examine the evidence used by each organization to support its viewpoint. Whose evidence is stronger and why? Cite the text in your answer.

2. Steve Connor thinks that cloning endangered species could help save some threatened animals, and Anna Jane Grossman thinks dog cloning isn't the worst thing that could happen to the dog population. However, Pete Shanks thinks both of these cloning pursuits cause animal suffering and are ethically wrong. Even though they have different viewpoints, there are some things the authors agree upon. List the issues that they agree upon and discuss how they can agree on these issues and still disagree about the acceptability of pet cloning or endangered species cloning.

Chapter 4

1. Leon R. Kass thinks reproductive and research cloning should be halted, while Christiane Nüsslein-Volhard thinks only reproductive cloning should be banned. Describe how each author views the beginning of life and how important it is to their viewpoint. Whose concept of the beginning of life do you agree with and why?

2. The US Food and Drug Administration contends it has studied cloned food and found it to be safe. However, Martha Rosenberg is not convinced that the FDA's evaluation is accurate. After reading both viewpoints, would you consume cloned meat or milk? Do you think cloned meat or milk should be labeled? Explain and support your answers using text from the viewpoints.

Organizations to Contact

The editors have compiled the following list of organizations concerned with the issues debated in this book. The descriptions are derived from materials provided by the organizations. All have publications or information available for interested readers. The list was compiled on the date of publication of the present volume; the information provided here may change. Be aware that many organizations take several weeks or longer to respond to inquiries, so allow as much time as possible.

Biotechnnology Industry Organization (BIO)
1201 Maryland Avenue SW, Suite 900, Washington, DC   20024
(202) 962-9200 • fax: (202) 488-6301
e-mail: info@bio.org
website: www.bio.org

The Biotechnology Industry Organization (BIO) provides advocacy, business development, and communications services for biotechnology businesses. The mission of BIO is to be the champion of biotechnology and the advocate for its member organizations. BIO hosts a number of meetings, such as the annual BIO International Convention, which brings biotechnology experts together. The organization provides many print and electronic publications and newsletters, including the *Bio News*.

Center for Bioethics & Human Dignity (CBHD)
Trinity International University, 2065 Half Day Road
Deerfield, IL   60015
(847) 317-8180 • fax: (847) 317-8101
e-mail: info@cbhd.org
website: www.cbhd.org

The Center for Bioethics & Human Dignity (CBHD) is a nonprofit organization established in 1994 in response to what was perceived as a lack of Christian input in the area of bioethics. CBHD promotes the potential contribution of biblical values in bioethical issues, such as stem cell research. The organization produces a wide range of resources examining bioethical issues, including "A Review of *Stem Cell Now: A Brief Introduction to the Coming Medical Revolution.*"

Center for Genetics and Society

1936 University Avenue, Suite 350, Berkeley, CA   94704
(510) 625-0819 • fax: (510) 665-8760
e-mail: info@geneticsandsociety.org
website: www.geneticsandsociety.org

The Center for Genetics and Society (CGS) is a nonprofit information and public affairs organization working to encourage responsible uses and effective societal governance of new human genetic and reproductive technologies. CGS supports benign and beneficent medical applications of the new human genetic and reproductive technologies, and it opposes those applications that objectify and commodify human life and threaten to divide human society. CGS provides many publications, including *Biopolitical Times* and *Weekly News & Views*.

Coalition for the Advancement of Medical Research (CAMR)

750 Seventeenth Street NW, Suite 1100
Washington, DC   20006
(202) 725-0339
e-mail: CAMResearch@yahoo.com.
website: www.camradvocacy.org

The Coalition for the Advancement of Medical Research (CAMR) was formed in 2001 to speak for patients, scientists, and physicians in the debate over stem cell research and the future of regenerative medicine. The group works to advance research and technologies in regenerative medicine, including embryonic stem cell research and somatic cell nuclear transfer (SCNT), in order to cure disease and alleviate suffering. The organization publishes various policy statements and facts about stem cell research and SCNT, including *Alternative Methods of Producing Stem Cells: No Substitute for Embryonic Stem Cell Research.*

Do No Harm: The Coalition of Americans for Research Ethics

1100 H Street NW, Suite 700, Washington, DC   20005

(202) 347-6840 • fax: (202) 347-6849

website: www.stemcellresearch.org

Do No Harm was founded by several scientists in July 1999 to oppose human embryonic stem cell research. The organization believes embryonic stem cell research is scientifically unnecessary, violates existing laws and policies, and is unethical. The organization acts as a clearinghouse for news and information on the dangers and failures of embryonic stem cells and the successes of alternative research. The organization publishes various fact sheets, background pieces, and reports related to stem cell research on its website, including *Diabetes Treatments: Adult Cells vs. Embryonic Stem Cells* and *Recent Advances in Adult Stem Cell Research and Other Alternatives to Embryonic Stem Cell Research/Cloning.*

Family Research Council—Center for Human Life and Bioethics

801 G Street NW, Washington, DC   20001

(202) 393-2100 • fax: (202) 393-2134

website: www.frc.org

The Family Research Council (FRC) is a Christian conservative nonprofit think tank and lobbying organization formed in 1981 by James Dobson. Its function is to promote what it considers to be traditional family values and socially conservative views on many issues, including divorce, homosexuality, abortion, and stem cell research. The FRC established the Center for Human Life and Bioethics in 1993 with the mission to inform and shape the public debate and to influence public policy to ensure the human person is respected in law, science, and society. The center publishes papers and other resources useful to the academic and political communities, as well as to the general public.

**Federation of American Societies
for Experimental Biology (FASEB)**
9650 Rockville Pike, Bethesda, MD   20814
(301) 634-7000 • fax: (301) 634-7001
e-mail: info@faseb.org
website: www.faseb.org

The Federation of American Societies for Experimental Biology (FASEB) was established in 1912 by three member societies. It currently consists of more than twenty societies, including the American Society for Biochemistry and Molecular Biology and the American Society of Human Genetics. The FASEB advances biological science through collaborative advocacy for research policies that promote scientific progress and education and lead to improvements in human health. The organization publishes a monthly peer-reviewed scientific research journal, *FASEB Journal*, and *Breakthroughs in Bioscience*, a series of illustrated essays that explain recent breakthroughs in biomedical research and how they are important to society.

Genetics Policy Institute (GPI)
11924 Forest Hill Boulevard, Suite 22
Wellington, FL   33414-6258
(888) 238-1423 • fax: (561) 791-3889
e-mail: bernard@genpol.org
website: www.genpol.org

The Genetics Policy Institute (GPI) promotes and advocates for stem cell research. Each year, GPI sponsors a World Stem Cell Summit, which brings together scientists and policy makers from around the world. The GPI publishes the presentations and views of those attending the summit in the annual World Stem Cell Summit report. Additionally, the GPI issues a monthly electronic newsletter with up-to-date stem cells news.

**National Institutes of Health Resource
for Stem Cell Research**
9000 Rockville Pike, Bethesda, MD   20892
(301) 496-4000

e-mail: stemcell@mail.nih.gov
website: http://stemcells.nih.gov/info/media/defaultpage.asp

The National Institutes of Health (NIH), a part of the US Department of Health and Human Services, is the primary federal agency for conducting and supporting medical research in the United States. The NIH is responsible for maintaining the NIH Human Embryonic Stem Cell Registry, which lists the derivations of stem cell lines eligible for federal funding. The NIH Stem Cell Information website provides various educational materials, facts, and scientific resources concerning stem cell research.

National Right to Life Committee
512 Tenth Street NW, Washington, DC   20004
(202) 626-8800
e-mail: NRLC@nrlc.org
website: www.nrlc.org

The National Right to Life Committee (NRLC) was founded in Detroit in 1973 in response to the US Supreme Court decision legalizing abortion. The NRLC is the largest pro-life organization in the United States. The group has local chapters in all fifty states and works to impact pro-life polices by lobbying the government at all levels. The group also serves as a clearinghouse of information and publishes the *National Right to Life News* on a periodic basis.

Presidential Commission for the Study of Bioethical Issues
1425 New York Avenue NW, Suite C-100
Washington, DC   20005
(202) 233-3960 • fax: (202) 233-3990
e-mail: info@bioethics.gov
website: www.bioethics.gov

The Presidential Commission for the Study of Bioethical Issues advises the president of the United States on bioethical issues that may emerge from advances in biomedicine and related areas of science and technology. The commission works

with the goal of identifying and promoting policies and practices that ensure that scientific research, health care delivery,
and technological innovation are conducted in an ethically responsible manner. The commission's blog is available at http://
blog.bioethics.gov/.

Bibliography of Books

George J. Annas   *American Bioethics: Crossing Human Rights and Health Law Boundaries.* New York: Oxford University Press, 2005.

Ronald Bailey   *Liberation Biology: The Scientific and Moral Case for the Biotech Revolution.* Amherst, NY: Prometheus Books, 2005.

Philip Ball   *Unnatural: The Heretical Idea of Making People.* London: Bodley Head, 2011.

Thomas C.G. Bosch, ed.   *Stem Cells: From Hydra to Man.* New York: Springer, 2008.

Sarah Franklin   *Dolly Mixtures: The Remaking of Genealogy.* Durham, NC: Duke University Press, 2007.

Joan Haran et al.   *Human Cloning in the Media: From Science Fiction to Science Practice.* New York: Routledge, 2008.

Judith A. Johnson and Erin D. Williams   *CRS Report for Congress: Stem Cell Research.* Washington, DC: Government Printing Office, 2006.

John Charles Kunich   *The Naked Clone: How Cloning Bans Threaten Our Personal Rights.* Westport, CT: Praeger, 2003.

Kerry Lynn Macintosh   *Illegal Beings: Human Clones and the Law.* New York: Cambridge University Press, 2005.

Jane Maienschein	*Whose View of Life?: Embryos, Cloning, and Stem Cells.* Cambridge, MA: Harvard University Press, 2003.
Steven P. McGiffen	*Biotechnology: Corporate Power Versus the Public Interest.* Ann Arbor, MI: Pluto, 2005.
Jonathan D. Moreno	*The Body Politic: The Battle over Science in America.* New York: Bellevue Literary Press, 2011.
Jonathan Morris	*The Ethics of Biotechnology.* Philadelphia, PA: Chelsea House Publishers, 2006.
National Research Council and Institute of Medicine	*Guidelines for Human Embryonic Stem Cell Research.* Washington, DC: National Academies Press, 2005.
Lars Østner, ed.	*Stem Cells, Human Embryos and Ethics: Interdisciplinary Perspectives.* New York: Springer, 2008.
Albert Sasson	*Medical Biotechnology: Achievements, Prospects and Perceptions.* New York: United Nations University Press, 2005.
Barry R. Schaller	*Understanding Bioethics and the Law: The Promises and Perils of the Brave New World of Biotechnology.* Westport, CT: Praeger, 2008.
George P. Smith II	*The Christian Religion and Biotechnology: A Search for Principled Decision-Making.* Norwell, MA: Springer, 2005.

Wendy Wagner and Rena Steinzor, eds. *Rescuing Science from Politics: Regulation and the Distortion of Scientific Research*. New York: Cambridge University Press, 2006.

Ian Wilmut and Roger Highfield *After Dolly: The Uses and Misuses of Human Cloning*. New York: W.W. Norton & Company, 2006.

John Woestendiek *Dog, Inc.: The Uncanny Inside Story of Cloning Man's Best Friend*. New York: Avery, 2010.

Index